THE WONGS
OF BELOIT, WISCONSIN

Lani Way drawing of Grandma Yee Shee Wong clamming. (Lani Way)

ﾑ〜

Clamming at Ocean Shores, Washington, with the Way Family by Lori Way
Galloway:

Grandma Wong would come out clamming with us, razor clamming. You dig
toward razor clams. And they dig away from you. They don't just sit there like
steamer clams. Razor clams have this foot. So they are digging away really fast! You
have this big old shovel....

I remember that Grandma would wear the traditional, the pointed Chinese cap,
for shade. I was really little, probably five or six. I was really scared because you see
in the cartoons that the clams come up and bite on your fingers. But Grandma
would put my hand down to show me how to catch the clams. She just loved it. She
was so happy clamming with us! Being at the ocean.

She had all this joy, I think, for a lot of things. This joy is about harvesting your
own food. We would cook it up and fry it up. You can tell from all of these stories
that food is so important in our family!

THE WONGS
OF BELOIT, WISCONSIN

BEATRICE LOFTUS MCKENZIE

THE UNIVERSITY OF WISCONSIN PRESS

Publication of this book has been made possible, in part, through support from the
Anonymous Fund of the College of Letters and Science at the University of Wisconsin–Madison.

The University of Wisconsin Press
728 State Street, Suite 443
Madison, Wisconsin 53706
uwpress.wisc.edu

Gray's Inn House, 127 Clerkenwell Road
London EC1R 5DB, United Kingdom
eurospanbookstore.com

Printed in the United States of America
This book may be available in a digital edition.

Library of Congress Cataloging-in-Publication Data
Names: McKenzie, Beatrice, author.
Title: The Wongs of Beloit, Wisconsin / Beatrice McKenzie.
Description: Madison, Wisconsin : The University of Wisconsin Press, [2022] | Includes bibliographical
references and index.
Identifiers: LCCN 2021021573 | ISBN 9780299335946 (paperback)
Subjects: LCSH: Wong family. | Chinese American families—Wisconsin—Beloit. | Immigrant families—
Wisconsin—Beloit. | Beloit (Wis.)—Biography.
Classification: LCC F590.C5 M35 2022 | DDC 977.5/87—dc23
LC record available at https://lccn.loc.gov/2021021573

This book is dedicated to the memory of
Yee Shee, "Mother Wong"

Contents

List of Illustrations   ix

Introduction   3

1 Transnational Migration in the Exclusion Era:
  Grandfather Wong Doo Set   11

2 Immigration and Settlement in Beloit:
  Charles Wong   33

3 Surviving and Thriving in Beloit:
  Yee Shee Wong   48

4 Family, Work, and Wartime Service:
  Gim, Fung, and George Wong   69

5 Part of a National Community:
  Helen, Harry, Frank, and Mary Wong   93

6 Family Reunions:
  Legacies and Advice for the Next Generations   131

Epilogue: Return to Mong Dee:
Mary Wong Palmer   146

Appendix   153

Notes   165

Index   193

Illustrations

Yee Shee Wong clamming at Ocean Shores, Washington   ii

Wong Doo Set, c. 1930   11

The Wong family ancestors (eight generations)   12

The Wong family (four generations)   13

Map of China showing Mong Dee, Duanfen, and Guangdong
province   15

Wong Ben Yuk from passport, 1888   18

Wong Ben Yuk after detention, 1889   19

Wong Doo Set's wife and children in China, 1922   31

Voyage from Mong Dee to San Francisco, c. 1909   34

Certificate of Identity of Wong Theong (a.k.a. Charles Wong), 1915   35

Yee Shee Gok and Charles Wong at wedding, 1913   36

Map showing Beloit, Wisconsin   38

Charles Wong's application for Yee Shee's immigration, 1923   43

Charles Wong, c. 1930   44

Charles Wong with car, 1930s   44

Yee Shee Wong, 1923   49

Yee Shee Gok with mother and sisters-in-law, 1913   50

Admiral Oriental Line brochure, 1923   54

Seattle to Chicago train route, 1923   55

Charles, Yee Shee, and Gim Wong, 1924   58

Beloit Hospital bill for Fung Wong's birth, 1926   58

Grandfather, Charles, Yee Shee, Bill, Ben, Gim, and Fung, c. 1928   59

Yee Shee Wong and children, 1935   61

Wong children, 1937   62

Wong family, 1950   64

Mother Yee Shee Wong, 1978   66

Gim Wong and George Wong, 1940s   72

Gim Wong and Mother Wong in Hong Kong, 1948   74

Gim and Marion Wong and children, 1968   76

Cadet Nurse program, U.S. Public Health Service, 1944   80

Fung Wong as nurse, 1947   81

Mother Wong and Alan Scholz, 1952   83

Fung, Al, Alan, Mary, and Cherie Scholz with cousins, 1975   84

Second Lieutenant George Wong, 1952   87

George Wong and Joyce Morrow correspondence, 1950s   88

Beloit Daily News clipping, 1969   90

George and Joyce Wong and children, 1970   91

Frank, Mary, and Helen Wong, 1944   95

Helen Wong, UW Madison, 1953   96

Helen and Jim Way and children, 1974   99

Chinese Cooking the Wong Way cookbook cover, 1977   100

Harry Wong, Beloit Memorial High School, 1951   103

Harry Wong anesthesia residency, Madison, 1960   106

Harry and Jean Wong and children in Hawaii, 1965   107

Harry Wong and extended family, 2018   110

Frank and Cynthia Wong wedding, 1967   112

Frank and Cynthia Wong and children, 1982   114

Mary Wong in Miss McKinley's first grade class at Royce
    School, 1943   121

Mary Wong in band uniform, 1953   122

Mary Wong in *Beloit Daily News* clipping, 1961   125

Mary and David Palmer and children, 1971   128

Yee Shee Wong and extended family, 1968   134

Frank in the box, 1982   135

Grandma's candy dish   141

Wong Reunion schedule, 2005   142

Mong Dee village gate, 2008   148

Farmer between banyan trees in Mong Dee, 2008   149

Mary Wong Palmer consulting oldest person in Mong Dee, 2008 150

THE WONGS
OF BELOIT, WISCONSIN

Introduction

My connection to the Wong family began in the Beloit College Archives in Beloit, Wisconsin, about ten years ago. A junior professor of U.S. history at Beloit College, I was conducting oral histories of alumni during a college reunion when the college archivist, Fred Burwell, introduced me to Mary Wong Palmer, whose connections to Beloit College went back decades. In our subsequent discussions, Mary asked me about doing research at the National Archives and Records Administration branch at San Bruno, California; years earlier I had researched Wong Kim Ark and his descendants there for my dissertation on the history of U.S. birthright citizenship policy.[1] Thus began a collaboration and warm friendship that resulted in the publication of this book.

The youngest of seven children, Mary Wong Palmer continued her siblings' lead in uncovering the family's history. As a child, Mary knew that her parents, Charles and Yee Shee Wong, emigrated from Guangdong province to Beloit, Wisconsin, early in the twentieth century to provide a better opportunity for their children. Her father had died when she was an infant and because her family did not openly discuss his death, she only learned that a Wong cousin had murdered her father when she asked her sister, Helen, about it when she was twelve years old. In the 1970s Helen Wong Way started the complicated process of unwinding the roots of their father's family by asking questions of older relatives. Helen sent out a genealogy survey to collect birth dates and spouses' names and to make a family tree for her father's family. In 1981 she and her brother, George, interviewed one of their grandfather's youngest children, Bob Wong.[2] Frank Wong and his wife,

Cynthia, also conducted research, asked questions of elders, and translated family records. Mary continued this research after Helen's and Frank's deaths, extending the research into her mother's family; she deepened it by writing to and interviewing many relatives in preparation for a trip to search for the family village, Mong Dee, in Guangdong, China, in 2008. After that trip, Mary collected additional immigration documents from the National Archives branches in San Bruno (NARA San Bruno) and Seattle (NARA Seattle) and visited sites relevant to the Wong family history in Seattle, San Francisco, and Ogden, Utah.

This is when I met Mary and our collaboration began. As a trained historian of the history of U.S. immigration and citizenship, I recommended some of the newest monographs on migration that could help her contextualize her family's history.[3] Mary wrote an account of the trip to China and Wong history that she later presented at a family reunion, and she brought the growing knowledge of her parents' history to my immigration history seminar at Beloit College later that year. We visited regularly, and Mary would update me on what she had learned about her family.

During this period I sought to incorporate local research into my academic career. My academic interest in Chinese immigration grew from experiences as a diplomat in the U.S. Foreign Service for five years and having lived in Tianjin, China, and Hong Kong for two years each in the early 1990s. At Beloit College I teach introductory courses on the history of U.S. citizenship and more advanced courses on U.S. immigration history. To understand local history better, I began to study the industrial history of Beloit, and I conducted oral history interviews with descendants of twentieth-century immigrant groups, including Eastern European and Latino immigrants, and Black migrants. In recognition of the value of this work, Beloit College named me Keefer Professor of Public Humanities in 2017.

In 2017 the Wong family approached me to write a history of their family during my upcoming sabbatical using the materials Mary had gathered. While they had in mind a self-published book, their story had greater relevance due to the lack of materials on Chinese immigrants to the Midwest and to Wisconsin, specifically.[4] Research and conference presentations on both the industrial globalization of the city of Beloit and the immigration of

Yee Shee and of her father-in-law helped make even more clear the academic significance of the family history and the work the Wongs had done to collect it.[5] In summer 2018 I systematically analyzed Mary's archival sources with Beloit College student Joanna Furlan.[6] We sought local school, college, newspaper, and corporation records from the Beloit College Archives, the Beloit Historical Society, the Rock County Historical Society, and the Wisconsin State Historical Society. Mary collected many materials on Wong family reunions, and Lisa Wong Fortsch, her niece, was willing to sort the materials into a coherent chronological record of family reunions. Beloit College students Aaron Kehuai Qiu translated several key documents in the family archival material and Pegg Stoddard conducted census research. That summer I visited NARA San Bruno to look for additional materials and study census records. I conducted secondary research and interviewed the surviving Wong siblings, Fung, Harry, and Mary.[7] In July 2018 I attended the Wong family reunion in Salt Lake City, where I interviewed twelve first cousins—Mary's children, nieces, and nephews—in addition to her brother Frank Wong's widow, Cynthia, and Mary's cousins, the Lees.[8] Full of the family spirit and optimism for the project, I determined the book's outline on the plane on the way home and drafted the manuscript during the 2019 spring semester. In addition to family members Mary Wong Palmer, Fung Wong Scholz, and Harry Wong, I am deeply indebted to scholars who read and offered suggestions to improve this work, especially Edward Mathieu, Torrie Hester, Ji-Yeon Yuh, Debra Majeed, Linda Sturtz, Kathryn White, and an anonymous reviewer for University of Wisconsin Press. Any errors that remain are, of course, my own.

Writing this book as a family memoir but with an academic audience in mind offered advantages and challenges. Unlike my previous research on Wong Kim Ark and his descendants, which relied heavily on government sources from NARA, this project used government sources extensively but also relied on family knowledge, recorded in the past and present. Family knowledge allowed certainty about the identity of family members. It also allowed for a greater reliance on certain immigration documents at NARA. We know, for example, that the documents Wong Ben Yuk filed for his sons Wong Mun Nging and Wong Mun Bin, in 1925, are reliable. Living and recently deceased family members have firsthand knowledge of the three men; Fung Wong Scholz, in particular, remembers when her step-uncles Mun Nging and Mun Bin lived with the family in Beloit for several years.[9] Family knowledge also helped solve a puzzle regarding the identity of the Wong grandfather, Wong Doo Set. While his grandchildren knew him to be an herbal doctor who practiced in Chicago, NARA records raised questions about his identity. They showed that he grew up—from the age of thirteen—as a cook on the West Coast of the United States but then declared himself to be a medical doctor at age thirty-eight, twenty-four years after immigrating. Separately, the surviving family members wondered why their Chinese American grandfather sponsored for citizenship several of his nephews but did not sponsor his eldest son, their father. A family interview cast new light on the paper documents (see chapter 1).

Relying on family sources poses challenges, too. In several areas an interviewee has interpreted events in their past in a different way than, for example, scholars in the field of Asian American studies would. As one example, when Harry Wong was hired as a teen in 1949 to work in the foundry at Fairbanks, Morse and Company in Beloit, Wisconsin, he became another of the men of color who, for decades, were relegated to that position. Interviews with and about Black migrants from the 1920s through the 1960s and newspaper articles about Italian workers in the 1910s indicate that northern industries used racialized workers in particular low-wage jobs through much of the twentieth century. Yet Harry himself does not believe his race affected the job he was placed in at Fairbanks.[10] While it seems clear that in an era when race was a key factor in matters as significant as admission to citizenship, it must also be evaluated as a deciding factor in job assignments.[11] Still, oral historians always walk a fine line between a source's identity and experiences and the academic's critical analysis.[12]

Beyond being true to the source, as a white author it is important to recognize and understand the many and complex ways the history of race in the United States plays out in each generation of the Wong family that I studied, as well as from my own subjectivity. It is possible that references to race, racism, or discrimination in oral interviews would be downplayed for a white scholar. This problem is intrinsic to oral history, especially when differences exist between the identities and positions of interviewer and interviewee. "Beyond the relationship of the oral historian and interviewee," immigration and public historian Mireya Loza points out, "the race, gender, class, and sexual orientation of the interviewer leaves legible marks on the recorded product."[13] I have sought to carefully clarify this aspect of analysis with Wong family members and the historical record.[14]

My collaboration with Mary Wong Palmer was one of many connections the Wong family has had to Beloit College, a liberal arts college of 1,300 students in the city of 37,000. In the middle of his academic career, between 1981 and 1987, Frank Wong served as dean and provost of the college. In that capacity, Frank started the first exchange relationship between Beloit College and Fudan University in Shanghai. Frank had had his first job—as a precocious twelve-year-old—compiling statistics of the college's winning basketball team for the *Beloit Daily News*. Two other Wong brothers, George and Gim, each attended Beloit College and lived at home for a year before transferring to the University of Wisconsin to study engineering. And Mary's husband, David Palmer, was the son of a faculty member and graduated from Beloit College. As a fitting end to this project, which draws heavily on Mary Wong Palmer's archive of family materials, the Beloit College Archives now houses that collection, which include copies of NARA documents and interviews, many original photographs, letters, legal documents, and memorabilia.[15]

This book tells the story of the Wong family; it is a story of immigrant determination, tragedy, resilience, and ultimately, community building. It is also a story of the attraction of the industrializing U.S. Midwest for Chinese immigrants and their children. Wong Theong (a.k.a. Wong Gwang Han), known locally as Charles or Charley Wong, moved with relatives from the West Coast to Beloit, Wisconsin, in 1920 to open and operate a restaurant that became a local institution, the Nan King Lo Restaurant, better known as the Chop House. Beloit is a small industrial city located one hundred miles northwest of Chicago on the main train lines between Chicago and its hinterlands in Wisconsin and Minnesota. The Wongs went to Chicago first. They may have left Chicago to seek opportunities in an era when the trend in chop suey houses spread beyond the largest cities, or they may have sought distance from immigration authorities. In Beloit, Charles purchased a home and brought his wife, Yee Shee, from China. The two had seven children between 1924 and 1937. Their children learned a mix of values from their parents and their neighbors, schools, and church; they became honor students, worked summer jobs, went to college, and became career professionals in several fields. Every one of the children went on to have a family, and their families remained close despite the distances that separated them. The Wong family history follows the contours of the transnational histories of Chinese Americans, first- and second-generation immigrants, the histories of the United States and of China in the late nineteenth and twentieth centuries, and the rise and fall of the industrial Midwest economy.[16]

The stories of Grandfather Wong Doo Set and his children (chapter 1) provide the background to the story of the Wongs in Beloit. This family is part of the ever-growing Wong family across the United States. The family would also shape and be shaped by life in Wisconsin. The next two chapters examine the biographies and immigration stories of two additional emigrants from Mong Dee: Wong Doo Set's eldest son, Wong Theong (Charles), and his wife, Yee Shee. Charles decided in 1920 to purchase a stake in a family restaurant in Beloit with his uncles. Chapter 2 examines Beloit's promising future in 1920, its recent industrial development and its migrant history, which included hundreds of recently arrived immigrants from southern and eastern Europe and African Americans from the South. Charles brought his wife, Yee Shee, from China and purchased a home on Lincoln Avenue in Beloit for their family. He carefully planned her voyage to prevent humiliating examinations and possible detention in the era of Chinese exclusion. Although Yee Shee spoke no English and rarely left their house, she set up a successful household and gave birth to seven children between 1924 and 1937. She forged relations with neighbors by sharing the bounty of the family's garden and fruit trees with them during the Depression. Charles's death in 1938 left Yee Shee to raise the children, ages one to fourteen, alone. Chapter 3 takes up Yee Shee's story, focusing on her upbringing, marriage, and emigration, and her life in Beloit after her husband's death. The only Chinese woman in the town, and one of a small number in the Midwest, Yee Shee's loss and isolation provoked a deep depression. The family persevered thanks to their own efforts and to excellent relationships with their neighbors, church community, and extended family members.

The second half of the book examines the lives of Yee Shee and Charles's children, second-generation Chinese Americans whose stories illustrate their opportunities and choices during World War II, the Cold War, and beyond. Chapter 4 examines the lives of the three elder Wong children, who came of age during World War II and who needed to stay close to their mother to help support her and the younger children. Two sons served in World War II and Korea, then attended the University of Wisconsin to become engineers; their careers progressed in the heyday of local industrial development and the service industry that accompanied that development. The eldest daughter was trained in wartime as a cadet nurse at the Madison General Hospital in Madison, Wisconsin; she later helped open the first emergency room at Beloit Hospital. These young people overcame overt racial discrimination, particularly when it came to their selection of marriage partners. Although Wisconsin was one of only nine states nationwide that never outlawed interracial marriage, each of the Wong children had an ugly experience of rejection by a suitor's family. The younger four children, the subjects of chapter 5, came of age in the early 1950s. They enjoyed expanded opportunities beyond the Midwest in the postwar globalized national economy. They formed identities within a hybridized set of Chinese American and European American cultural expectations and through interactions with more Chinese, Asian American, and international individuals and groups outside the Midwest.

Chapter 6, which functions as a conclusion, examines the ways that the Wong siblings maintained close relations and conveyed their values to the following generations. A series of letters that rotated through the families details the joys and challenges of raising children in the 1960s and 1970s. Grandmother Wong remained in Beloit with her three elder children, who continued to work for flagship Beloit industries even as opportunities in the Midwest dried up for their children. Family reunions allowed the children raised in the Midwest to bond with their cousins from the East and West Coasts. An epilogue offers a glimpse of Mong Dee village in Taishan county of Guangdong province in 2008, when family members returned to visit.

The Wong family of Beloit, Wisconsin, thrived in spite of dramatic set-backs. Their immigrant parents transmitted strong and traditional Chinese values of courage, honor, respect for elders, and hard work. They learned American values of industriousness, achievement, and community building from neighbors, teachers, and employers in the place their parents chose to settle—Beloit, Wisconsin. Even after the violent death of their father, the second-generation Chinese American family grew with a strong sense of solidarity and community. The family's biography is complex, involving themes of transnational migration, race, national law, local and regional economic development, and the construction of communities in Beloit and within an extended family. This is their story.

CHAPTER ONE

Transnational Migration in the Exclusion Era

Grandfather Wong Doo Set

The Wong siblings share a memory of playing around their grandfather in the summertime as he sat in his rocking chair, wheezing, in the living room of their home in Beloit.[1] Wong Doo Set was a medical doctor who practiced in Chicago. Every summer, when his asthma flared in the hot and humid weather, he used to stay with his son and family in Beloit, Wisconsin.[2] In addition to offering an introduction to the Wong family patriarch and several puzzles around his identity, Wong Doo Set's story offers an overview of Chinese emigration in the late nineteenth and early twentieth centuries, when racist laws severely restricted Chinese immigration to the United States.

Grandfather Wong Doo Set's photo hung in the living room at 1015 Lincoln, c. 1930. (WFP, Beloit College Archives)

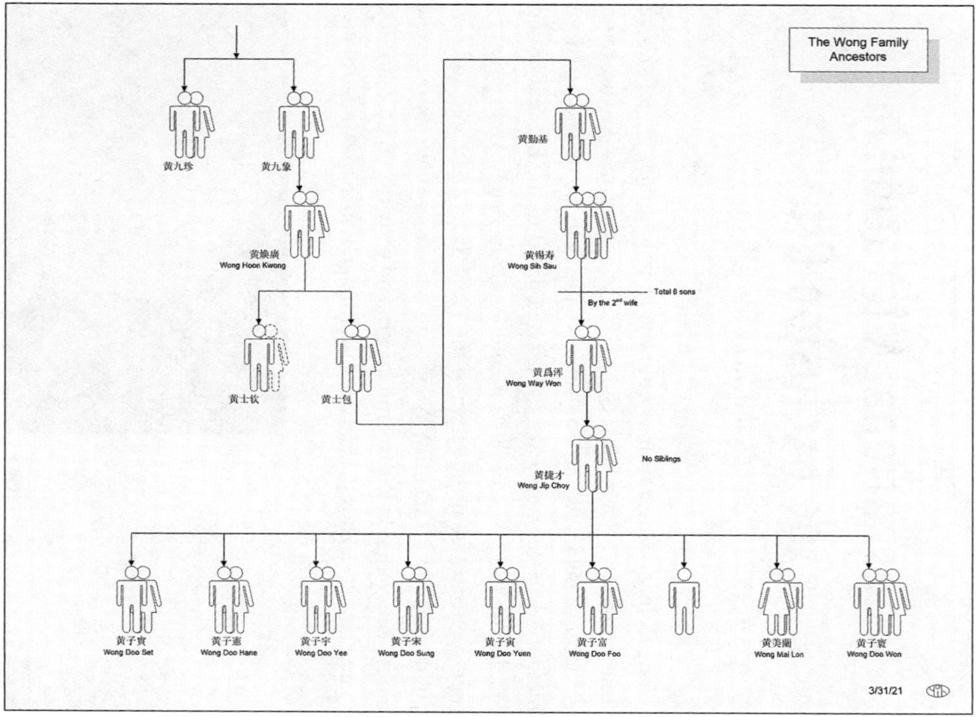
The Wong Family Ancestors
黄九珍
黄九象
黄焕廣
Wong Hoon Kwong
黄士钦
黄士包
黄勤基
黄锡寿
Wong Sih Sau
Total 6 sons
By the 2nd wife
黄爲浑
Wong Way Won
黄捷才
Wong Jip Choy
No Siblings
黄子實
Wong Doo Set
黄子憲
Wong Doo Hane
黄子宇
Wong Doo Yee
黄子宋
Wong Doo Sung
黄子寅
Wong Doo Yuen
黄子富
Wong Doo Foo
黄美蘭
Wong Mai Lon
黄子賨
Wong Doo Won
3/31/21

The Wong family ancestors (eight generations). (Bob Yih)

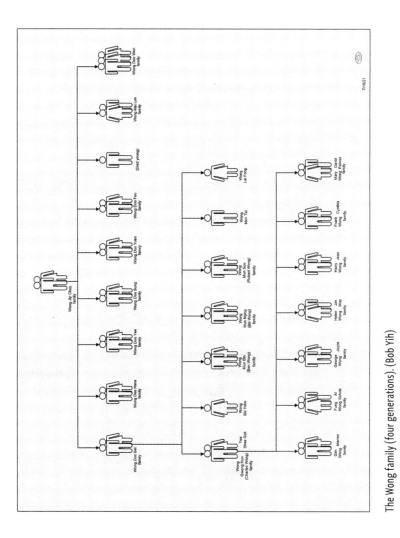

The Wong family (four generations). (Bob Yih)

A Question of Identity: Wong Doo Set and Wong Ben Yuk

Doo Set came from a well-established family in China, one whose Han ancestors originated in Northern China and moved south in the centuries preceding the nineteenth. Doo Set was the eldest of eight sons in his family, a position that, following Chinese Confucian tradition, conveyed status, inheritance rights, and obligations to younger brothers and nephews.

Doo Set's life story intersects with that of his brother Ben Yuk in a surprising way. Doo Set came to the United States in 1912 in place of his younger brother, Wong Ben Yuk (a.k.a. Wong Doo Hane), and his true identity was nearly lost to his descendants. Wong Doo Set was in many ways a typical Chinese emigrant in the early twentieth century. Chinese emigrants in that era often left their villages in what is called stage migration, moving at different stages of their lives to multiple destinations. Doo Set was born in 1870 in Mong Dee village in Taishan county, Guangdong.[3] The village of Mong Dee was near Duanfen township, on the Pearl River Delta, an active trade route with connections to broader trade in the region and beyond. Mong Dee was an emigrants' village (*qiaoxiang*), a village from which many boys and young men departed to find work. The emigrants found work elsewhere and sent earnings back to their families.[4] Doo Set attended three years of school in his village, then left home for Guangzhou at the age of ten, likely continuing to study and then to work as an apprentice to an herbal doctor. The age at which he left indicates Doo Set was selected to learn a profession and was expected to bring medical knowledge back to a practice in or near the village. It was the boys' fathers and other male relatives who selected which sons should go forth from the village and where and with whom they should land.[5] His elders likely judged Doo Set to have an aptitude for medicine. In China, this meant the ability to master the medical knowledge, access supplies, and especially to interact with individuals at all levels of society. His story, like that of many other young boys, formed a part of the broader history of emigration from Southern China.

The record was righted only recently with the discovery of two pieces of evidence. Both were hidden away in an interview that had taken place at a Wong family reunion in 1982, which was captured on a cassette tape. All

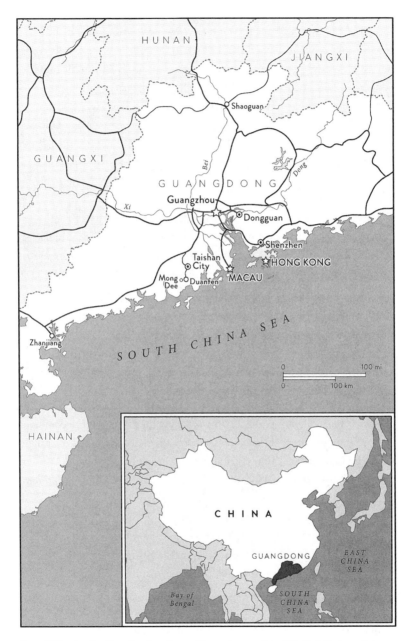

Map of China showing Mong Dee, Duanfen, and Guangdong province. (Erin Greb Cartography)

three persons speaking on the tape are now deceased, and the conversation had not previously been transcribed. In the 1982 interview, Bob Wong, one of Doo Set's youngest sons, was translating notes left by his father—apparently notes he had used to prepare for his entries as a U.S. citizen. In annotations to those notes, Doo Set admitted to taking over his younger brother's papers. He said that he added his married name, Wong Doo Set, to the list of aliases so that his children would remember who their father was. He also explained that three of the four "oldest sons" he had sponsored were in fact his younger brother's sons.[6] Bob Wong said on the tape that his relatives in China had confirmed this story.

We are not sure how this impersonation was accomplished. Although Doo Set resembled his brother when they were young, the change in his features evident in the photographs in his immigration file from 1908 and 1912 could not be explained merely by aging. The paper record indicates that Doo Set, who had a prosperous medical practice in his home region and traveled frequently to Guangzhou and Hong Kong, was of a higher social class—more educated, wealthy, and cosmopolitan, not to mention literate—than Wong Ben Yuk. From 1888 to 1908 Ben Yuk claimed to be a cook, but on his fourth trip, in 1912, the thirty-eight-year-old stated that he was a medical doctor. In 1912 U.S. immigration officials had doubts about Ben Yuk. They were not sure that he was the same man who had arrived four years earlier. Yet in his responses to immigration officials, the older brother was far more confident than his younger brother had ever been. For the first time in the record, he signed his name using Chinese characters, and in 1912 his signature in Western characters improved dramatically. Furthermore, his photo looked different. Immigration officials did an investigation that involved a lengthy interview and study of two photographs and, somewhat surprisingly, they determined that he *was* the same person. As happened in other documented cases, it is likely that the immigration official recognized and was deferential to Doo Set's evident class status and assumed the successful herbal doctor was the citizen despite the discrepancy in appearance.[7]

This new information helped resolve several inconsistent or puzzling elements of Wong Doo Set's story and reveals much about the history of migration during the era of Chinese exclusion. The case of the Wong family is emblematic of the ways that families migrating had to navigate around the U.S. regime of Chinese exclusion, often making nephews and cousins into sons, and sons into the offspring of others—at least on paper. Grandfather Wong brought eight sons to the United States, but two of the first three he sponsored are known to the family to be his nephews. And he sent a man we definitely know to be his son, Charles, to the United States as the son of another man.

The Path Forged by Wong Ben Yuk

As we have seen, Grandfather Wong was not the first in his family to go to the United States. If he is now recognized as the patriarch of his family in the United States, it is thanks to the path laid out by his younger brother, the second eldest son, Wong Ben Yuk (a.k.a. Wong Doo Hane). While the Wong grandfather, Doo Set, learned his medical trade in a cosmopolitan Chinese city, the family sent his brother, Ben Yuk, to the United States.

In 1888 thirteen-year-old Wong Ben Yuk rode in steerage class to the United States on board the Pacific Mail steamship *Gaelic*, planning to claim his right to land as a citizen of the United States.[8] His arrival and experiences from September to April 1889 were traumatic. Ben Yuk arrived during one of the most contentious political moments of the anti-Chinese period, just prior to the passage of the bill, in October 1888, that ended what immigration restrictionists claimed was a loophole in an earlier Chinese restriction law. Too many passengers from China were claiming, without certificates to prove it, that they were permanent residents of the United States. Customs inspectors doubted Ben Yuk's claim to have been born in San Francisco in 1874, and they left him detained by the shipping company with dozens of other Chinese men and boys from the same steamer. The detention center on Angel Island had not yet been built. In the 1880s, immigrants who were not allowed to land were detained by immigration officials on the ship they arrived in. If the company needed that ship, newcomers could be transferred to another ship or to a warehouse. The shipping company housed between 200 and 400 Chinese detainees at a time in a dingy two-story wooden structure at First and Brannan Streets in San Francisco. None of these holding spaces were considered to be "on U.S. soil," leaving the migrants suspended in spaces that were not defined as part of the nation.[9] Housing conditions were inadequate, but Ben Yuk's detention held other horrors.

U.S. government officials boarded the *Gaelic* soon after it arrived in the harbor. Previous transpacific voyages in 1887 and 1888 had been marred by out-breaks of smallpox, requiring quarantine of the passengers.[10] Since so many voyagers wished to make the trip before the entry restrictions hardened, the shipping company crowded an excess number of voyagers on board. Over-crowded conditions, in turn, exacerbated the smallpox outbreaks. As the ship landed, both health and immigration officers boarded to inspect the pas-sengers. Although officials knew beforehand which passengers had "Canton certificates"—the prearranged immigration documents that allowed for the return of permanent residents—many more passengers lacked these certifi-cates than had them. In response to the query for documents, Ben Yuk asked the officer to contact the one person in San Francisco who knew he had lived there: Wong Sang.[11] Just saying the man's name must have predisposed author-ities toward his case, for Ben Yuk was not immediately returned to China. The stakes of those initial decisions were very high for immigrants. One young

Wong Ben Yuk's 1888 passport photo, taken before he left China, age 13. (30734/3-23 WONG Ben Yuk file, NARA San Bruno)

Chinese man in detention with Ben Yuk was not so fortunate: scheduled to be returned to China, that young man became so despondent about the outcome of his case that he hanged himself.[12] That is how young Ben Yuk's detention began. He was then held on board a ship and in the detention shed with hundreds of other boys and men from September 1888 to April 1889. Photos of the boy taken before and after detention tell a story of much hardship. In addition to witnessing the young shipmate who committed suicide, he and others suffered overcrowding, lack of food, and unhygienic conditions.

In March 1888 Ben Yuk's habeas corpus case came before Judge Ogden Hoffman in the District Court for California's Northern District. Although Hoffman expected Wong Sang would vouch for Wong Ben Yuk's previous status as a permanent resident in the United States, Wong Sang went further, stating that he knew of Ben Yuk's birth in the country, meaning he was a U.S. citizen. Birth in the United States conveys the right to enter the country. With an order that recognized Ben Yuk's U.S. birthright citizenship, Hoffman commanded his release on April 8, 1889.[13]

Wong Ben Yuk's photo taken in April 1889, after six months of detention in San Francisco. (30734/3-23 WONG Ben Yuk file, NARA San Bruno)

After gaining admission to the United States, Ben Yuk traveled back and forth to China several times over the next few years, each time having to go through the immigration inspections. He arrived in the United States again in 1896 at age twenty-two and in 1903 at age twenty-nine.[14] It is not clear exactly where he lived in the United States during this period, although he told immigration officials in 1903 that he had worked in Oakland, California, as a cook for a Mr. Treadwell, on 49th Street, "for a long, long time."[15] At some point, Ben Yuk moved from California to Chicago. The 1903 landing may have been his opportunity to move there, for the Chinese community in Illinois was expanding, and leaders of the community, also from Guangdong, invited their brethren currently in California to join them.

The question of whether Ben Yuk was or was not born in the United States introduces the issue of primary sources for this book and for Chinese immigration history more broadly. This book draws on immigration and court records from the National Archives, local newspapers, and family letters and photos. There exists a thick file on Ben Yuk's initial immigration interview and documents from his subsequent journeys. Even though a court record confirms Ben Yuk's birth in the United States, which is based on the testimony of Wong Sang, the thirteen-year-old may have been instructed by his family to claim U.S. citizenship on the understanding that this was what was required of him to enter the country. Another major source for the project is family interviews, admittedly of the generations following Ben Yuk's. No interviewee suggested that Ben Yuk truly *was* born in the United States. Oral histories conducted in 1982 and 2018 suggest no memory or discussion of travel by the preceding generation or births in the United States.[16] Wherever he *was* born, however, Ben Yuk's significance to the family is paramount. He is the source that allowed generations of Wongs to immigrate and ultimately to establish themselves in the United States.

An Emigrant from Guangdong Province (Wong Ben Yuk)

Emigration as a communal tactic in nineteenth-century China had a long history. Rooted in earlier dynasties, when regions specialized in particular goods, some young men would be sent to another district to carry on the regional specialty in places where it did not yet exist. These were not impoverished immigrants desperately seeking food and shelter. Choosing to relocate to another region or abroad was a strategy a family followed to increase its wealth. This "mobility strategy" resulted in large numbers of Chinese men pursuing occupations far from home, often in more urban places, while maintaining homes back in their ancestral villages.[17] Family decision-makers would groom one son to stay home and take care of the women and children and handle the remittances sent from abroad while the other sons, when they reached the age of about fourteen, would be sent to a distant city to stay with a relative or friend of the family.[18] There, they would be taken on as an apprentice, with free room and board, for about three years. After the apprenticeship, the young man would be sent home for a three-month vacation during which time he would marry. The cycle would begin anew when he left his wife in his home village and returned to work in the same or a new urban area.[19]

Wong Ben Yuk spent decades as a cook at various job sites in California. He traveled back to China several times. On one of his trips he married a woman named Yee Shee (not to be confused with the Yee Shee that his nephew, Charles, married; Yee Shee was a common name for young women of the region), and he took on the married name Wong Doo Hane. Tragedy struck on a later visit to China. During a flu epidemic that ravaged Guangdong region at some point between 1908 and 1912, Ben Yuk and three of his sons died. After his death, his older brother, the herbal doctor Wong Doo Set, began impersonating his brother for immigration purposes. Wong Doo Set—or Grandfather Wong—made his first trip to the United States in 1912.[20]

The emigration of boys and young men from the Taishan region, Guangdong in the late nineteenth century had particular demographic roots. The population of China had increased dramatically during the Qing Dynasty (1644–1912), doubling from 150 to 300 million between 1650 and 1800 and then growing to 450 million by 1850. Han Chinese who emigrated from the north to this part of China over centuries eventually ran short of arable land on which to farm, cut wood, or practice trades. Population density and land scarcity meant that as many as one-quarter of the men in the late nineteenth century Taishan region needed to seek work elsewhere, whether in another city or region in China or overseas.[21]

Chinese also emigrated to manage risk in an era of pronounced political instability. The population of the Taishan region experienced upheaval in the wake of European colonialism in the nineteenth and twentieth centuries. Following the lead of the Portuguese and the Dutch, the British enlarged their empire in the East, conquering India at the turn of the nineteenth century and expanding their markets for industrial raw materials and labor. How they accomplished this is a complicated story of tea, opium, coercion, and military strength. At the turn of the nineteenth century, the British founded settlements in Penang and Singapore as way stations en route to China. Tea became such a significant product for the British that the trade balance favored the Chinese, so the British—and soon the American traders, too—began to traffic opium grown in India to China to pay for the tea. By the 1830s, the trade balance had shifted, and China and Great Britain fought the Opium Wars in 1840–1842 and 1856–1860. Following its defeat, China signed a series of treaties with Britain, France, and the United States, known as the "unequal treaties," which were pacts that forced the Chinese to accept encroachments by Western governments. The British government demanded an indemnity of $21 million; they acquired Hong Kong; and they exacted the use of five "treaty ports" on or near the eastern coast of China between Shanghai and Guangzhou that would be opened to foreign trade. The unequal treaties also resulted in higher taxes levied on Chinese peasants. Domestic dislocation and volatility followed all of these pressures; four rebellions in the nineteenth century alone led to the deaths of 20 million Chinese.[22] At various moments in this era of Western imperialism, Chinese sought to leave their country as short-term sojourners, economic migrants, and as refugees fleeing war.

Chinese Immigration to the United States, Race, and the Chinese Exclusion Act

Chinese immigrated to the United States as one of several overseas destinations in the Western Hemisphere. Well before the nineteenth century, hundreds of thousands of Chinese and other Asians had migrated to Latin America and the British West Indies, and a smaller number had gone to Canada and the East Coast of the United States.[23] But the West Coast, and specifically California, was the most important U.S. destination for Chinese emigrants. By 1877 148,000 out of a total of 200,000 Chinese who immigrated to the United States went to California.[24] Decades into the migration, in 1910, the United States built an immigration reception station on Angel Island in San Francisco Bay. Tens of thousands of Chinese migrated to the United States as miners and service laborers during the California Gold Rush (1848) and as railroad workers on the Transcontinental Railroad (1865–1869). In 1867, 90 percent of the railroad laborers on the western side of the Transcontinental Railroad route were Chinese.[25] Chinese also labored in factories in San Francisco, as farmers and agricultural workers on the West Coast, and on sugar plantations in Hawaii. Many came for economic opportunities; others came in search of education or freedom from persecution. By 1880 there were more than 300,000 Chinese in the United States, and although two-thirds of the Chinese immigrants lived in California, over the next two decades they spread out to big cities and small towns across America.[26]

Trade and missionary work were critical elements of the U.S.–Chinese relationship that shaped U.S. immigration policy toward the Chinese. In the era of British hegemony in China, from the 1840s to the 1890s, the United States had insisted that it be included in the semi-colonial China trade. When the United States replaced Great Britain as the global hegemonic power in the early twentieth century, historian Yoneyuki Sugita argues that its "open door policy" sought an imprimatur of moral superiority over European principles while it maintained China's territorial integrity. Its true intent was not benevolent, however, but rather to protect access to the entire Chinese market for American traders. As was the case in the British system that preceded it, whatever trade concessions China made to any of the European countries would also apply to all other most favored nations, including the United States.[27] A second aspect of the relationship that affected U.S. policy toward Chinese immigrants was the presence of American missionaries in China. Having first proselytized in China in the 1830s, by the early twentieth century there were about one thousand American missionaries throughout China. While some aspects of the missionary presence were truly benevolent, Chinese historian (and Wong family member) Frank Wong pointed out in his research that the missionaries' "real contribution to China" was "the subversion of the traditional culture."[28] As Wong explained, the missionaries' spiritual calling reinforced a widespread American belief that the United States had both a right and responsibility to "civilize" China—a belief very similar to that of "Manifest Destiny," which drove settlement of the western United States by Anglo-Americans. Their calling to serve in China also depended upon their belief that Chinese were "barbarous to begin with, [and that they lacked] art and literature, political order, and social morality."[29] Chinese fought these stereotypes in violent uprisings against foreign missionaries, such as the anti-imperialist and anti-Christian Boxer Rebellion in Beijing in 1900, which was defeated by an eight-nation Western military force. The weakened state of the Qing government in this era helped reinforce Western notions that Chinese civilization was in decline due to the moral failings of its population. In the last decades of the nineteenth century, U.S. policy toward Chinese immigrants reflected this complicated relationship. The United States would seek to continue access to the China trade and entrée and security for American missionaries in China while it prevented the mass migration of Chinese to the United States.

In 1882 Congress restricted the immigration of Chinese laborers in the first of a series of laws known as the Chinese Exclusion Act. A violent, virulently racist anti-Chinese social movement had emerged in California in the 1860s and 1870s. Leaders of the movement claimed that "'Oriental Civilization' was incompatible with the U.S. and threatened to corrupt the nation."[30] A second charge was that Chinese labor undercut white workers. In the 1870s nearly half the working men employed in shoe, textile, and cigar factories in San Francisco were Chinese. They were paid less than their white counterparts, drawing the charge by white laborers that Chinese laborers represented unfair competition.[31] "Chinese exclusion" refers to the set of laws that were in effect between 1882 and 1943, which set up an almost total ban on immigration from China.

In the following decades, the exclusion was extended and applied to other groups from Asia. These laws remained in effect and, in 1917, Congress drew an imaginary line—called the Asiatic barred zone—through the Pacific Ocean. Laborers from the other side of the line could be excluded at will when they sought entry to the United States. The Chinese Exclusion Act marked the first time in American history that the United States barred a group of immigrants because of their nationality, race, and social class.[32] Small exceptions to the overall ban allowed Christian ministers, students, and wealthy Chinese traders to enter. In the 1880s there was an exception for laborers who could show that they had already established permanent residence in the United States, using a form they acquired before they left called a "Canton certificate." If the person arriving claimed permanent residence and did not have a certificate, they could bring to an immigration hearing someone from the Chinese community who would vouch for their long-term resident status. There was one other category of legal entry and that was entry as a United States citizen.

Chinese American children, whether born in the United States or born to U.S. citizens abroad, were in a privileged category. For many years American nativists tried to prevent the children of Chinese immigrants who were born in the United States from claiming birthright citizenship, an issue that was settled ten years after Ben Yuk's first trip. Federal courts consistently rejected the racist effort. In 1898 the U.S. Supreme Court ruled that Wong Kim Ark, who had been born in San Francisco in 1870 to Chinese immigrant parents, was a citizen at birth, "regardless of race."[33] This ruling affirmed that— as was the case for children of other American fathers—Chinese born in the United States and children born to Chinese Americans abroad could claim birthright U.S. citizenship.[34] The Beloit Wong forbears similarly claimed they had been born in the United States.

The expansive birthright citizenship policy alongside the restrictive immigration policy led to a phenomenon known as "paper sons." Paper sons were fictive children of Chinese American fathers. During the centuries that Chinese men from southern and southeastern China had departed their homeland to work abroad, they most often left their wives and children in their home villages. In the mid-nineteenth century, most Chinese men who traveled to North America continued this practice, although some Chinese (like the parents of Wong Kim Ark of the Supreme Court case) did immigrate as husband and wife. The men who traveled abroad as sojourners earned money and built lives abroad, but they remitted their earnings and returned home every few years and ultimately intended to repatriate to China. Beginning in the 1880s but especially after 1906, when an earthquake and fire destroyed birth records in San Francisco, many Chinese who had been prevented from immigrating by Chinese exclusion claimed to have been born in the United States. Some of them gave or sold their papers to others who hoped to get their sons jobs in California or elsewhere in the United States. The Immigration Bureau tried to end this fraudulent practice by detaining Chinese immigrants in harsh conditions, interviewing fathers and sons, and calling in witnesses to swear to relationships.

Wong Doo Set availed himself of the "child of a citizen" loophole in the Chinese exclusion laws and claimed several children who were not his actual sons, alongside several children who were. His case is instructive of the "paper son" phenomenon. In the same way that relatives determined which sons would remain in the village and which would venture forth, families also thought of immigration slots in a communal way. Thus, although Doo Set brought several children who were not his own to the United States, we have reason to believe that all but one of the persons he brought were related to him.[35] If they were not his actual sons, they were his brothers' sons.

Wong Doo Set in the Chicago Chinese Community

One important factor in the Wong family story is the place of industrializing Chicago as a regional hub for the midwestern Chinese community. Scholarship about Chicago and its hinterlands focuses on its role as an engine of growth for the national economy at the turn of the twentieth century. Its access to water and transportation—specifically the railroads that headed both east and west—made it a locus for national and international trade before 1880. By 1889 it was America's second largest city. The city grew dramatically during and after the Civil War; between 1880 and 1910 Chicago saw a 330 percent growth of population to work its industries in iron and steel manufacturing, machinery, chemicals, and food processing.[36] Chicago attracted Chinese who were eager to leave the West Coast at the same time as Chicago was industrializing. As historian Adam McKeown writes, "the Eastern United States was attractive to new [Chinese] migrants in the early twentieth century because it offered more opportunities for people with little capital and skill to open small, independent businesses."[37]

During the first decades of the twentieth century, the Chicago Chinese community comprised Chinese from the south of China, like the Wongs, and others from the north. The southern Chinese, a much larger group, were less educated, poorer, and more likely to be engaged in opium smoking and gambling. They spoke Cantonese, a language that uses the same written form but is unintelligible to speakers of several other Chinese dialects, including Mandarin Chinese. After 1900 a number of Chinese came to Chicago to study at the University of Chicago and Northwestern as "indemnity students." The indemnity that China paid for anti-Western violence during the Boxer Rebellion covered the tuition for many Chinese students in the United States.[38] From elite families in China, these students spoke Mandarin Chinese and had ties to more established political and intellectual circles. They looked down on the southern Chinese. One student, for example, dismissively described Chicago's Chinatown in 1924 this way: "This can hardly be termed a community as there are only eight or nine shops kept by the Cantonese. . . . Groups of apparent idlers are seen sitting in some of the larger shops sipping tea and gossiping. The total absence of women and children from the street or the shop window is strikingly remarkable."[39] The quote, which helps us visualize the Chinese community in Chicago, nevertheless shows the student's misunderstanding of its formation.

Several people interviewed in the 1920s spoke of the division of the Chicago Chinese into two "parties" after the 1911 Chinese Revolution. The politically more conservative group was better off and less inclined to take offense when Clark Street landlords raised rents on Chinese to drive them out. This conservative group was more willing to withstand racial hostility, keep their heads low, and make money in their restaurants and laundries in various locations throughout the city. The other party, with more progressive and more nationalist views toward China, moved to Chinatown and organized benevolent groups to provide service to Chinese immigrants.[40]

A visiting Chinese diplomat had suggested to the growing community of about six hundred in the late 1880s that they spread out across the city rather than congregate in the area along Clark Street that was already being referred to as Chinatown. The 1890 census showed evidence of dispersal: only two out of seventeen wards in Chicago had no Chinese residents, and five wards had between thirteen and forty-eight residents each.[41] The integration camp also viewed the Chicago Columbian Exposition of 1893 as an opportunity for their community to gain acceptance.

Chinese businessmen and leading immigrants in Chicago decided to organize a Chinese village at the World's Fair, in part to combat a negative view of the Chinese among Anglo-Americans. In protest of the 1882 and 1892 Chinese Exclusion Acts, the Chinese Empress Dowager had declined to send an official delegation to the exhibition; so three Chicago Chinese businessmen organized a Chinese Pavilion with entertainment, shopping, and food on the Midway Plaisance. The three were widely praised by the Chicago press for their business savvy and Western lifestyles. They hoped their café and teahouse would provide a venue for their interaction with white middle-class fairgoers. The café may have been the "first Americanized Chinese restaurant in the Midwest," although beyond tea and sweets, the menu offerings seemed mainly to be Euro-American.[42] This model, however, proved effective for Chinese in other towns and cities across the United States in the twentieth century.

The successful teahouse at the Chicago World's Fair sparked a second strategy for gaining acceptance into American society in Chicago, which was to use Chinese restaurants to interact with the American public at large.[43] One of the first restaurants in Chicago, the King Joy Lo Mandarin Restaurant, drew Chicago's elite to its elegant tables. Opened in 1905, the restaurant was located at Dearborn and Randolph, in the Theater District. Several other fine dining establishments opened on Clark Street, and more homey chop suey restaurants opened throughout the city. As Chinese restaurants flourished in Chicago between 1893 and 1902, Chinese in Chicago encouraged their relatives on the West Coast to relocate.[44] The Wongs likely heard this call.

Outside of the memory of his grandchildren, there are scant formal records that confirm Wong Doo Set's residence or place of business in Chicago.[45] Family history places his sons Bob and Tai as primary school students at the Haines Public School near Chinatown in the early 1930s.[46] In the 1920s and 1930s, when the Wong children were small, they remember fondly many visits from their grandfather. At that point he worked as an herbal doctor in

Chicago. His asthma brought him to Beloit in the summertime, where he enjoyed the cool breezes on the back porch.

Doo Set was married twice, and both wives remained in China. His first wife, Charles's mother, died in China in 1909.[47] When Doo Set remarried, however, his wife gave birth to several other children who were Charles's half-siblings. Doo Set often stated that he "brought all of his sons to the United States" by 1931.[48]

Perils of Transnational Success Back in the Village

In contrast to the lack of evidence of formal residency in Chicago, Doo Set's residency in the United States and the resulting lives of his extended family enabled them to make a lasting mark back in China. Markers of the success of Doo Set and his younger brothers and sons were visible in their village in 1921, in the construction of new brick homes and buildings in an adjacent part of the village they called the New Village. In an immigration interview on behalf of his sons' entry in 1925, Doo Set described with pride his house and a large public building that functioned as a social hall and that he also used as his doctor's office.[49] His new house was a "regular five-room house with an open (courtyard) and tile floors."[50] The house was illuminated by coal-oil lamps—one large lamp suspended in the parlor and others that could be carried into other rooms as needed. A pendulum clock brought from the United States in 1921 hung in the parlor. The new house also had a shrine shelf and five ancestral tablets that were green with gold letters—signs of wealth that "commemorated Doo Set's father, his grandfather, and other ancestors." Although there was no sign advertising Doo Set's medical practice, there was "fancy work" lettering above the outside entrance of the social hall, which read, "Om Hing Wong Ancestral Hall."[51]

This wealth drew bandits to Mong Dee village, causing a shift in the family's long-term strategy. Doo Set had arrived home to Mong Dee in May 1921 (where he remained until 1925), and he completed the new construction of his familial compound that November. He was away many nights conducting business in Guangzhou and Sun Chung City and making medical calls closer to home. In his absence bandits raided the village several times. In 1924 they raided the school at midnight, kidnapped all thirty students, and held them for ransom for six months. Since only boys attended the school, no girls were taken. However, the bandits also took the teacher and four adult watchmen, killing one of them. This episode undoubtedly contributed to Doo Set's decision to bring two sons back to the United States with him the following year, even though they were still quite young.

In April 1925 Doo Set returned to the United States from China, bringing his sons Mun Bin (Ben) and Mun Nging (Bill) with him. The boys were only ten and twelve years old, and they had not yet completed the three years of schooling in Mong Dee that the other Wong children had. The boys spent a short time in detention at Angel Island, but they were able to make their citizenship case, as sons born abroad to a U.S. citizen father, relatively quickly and were released in early May. By September they were living with their older half-brother, Charles, and his wife, Yee Shee, in Beloit, Wisconsin. Both started first grade at nearby Royce School having shaved two years off their ages. School records show that the boys began the year with no English, and thus failed English class the first semester. But they had become proficient by June 1926, a bit more than a year after they arrived in the United States.[52] Their attendance, best in their class, suggested both excellent health and an organized household. Their sister-in-law, Yee Shee, would have had only one child when they arrived, though she gave birth to their niece Fung several months later. In all, Ben completed two years of schooling at Royce (possibly leaving when it became apparent that he was an adolescent heading into third grade), and Bill completed fifth grade there. In 1929, when his nephew Gim started kindergarten, fifth-grader Bill walked him to school.[53]

Doo Set brought two of his youngest sons—nine-year-old twins Wong Mun Tai (Tai) and Wong Mun Soo (Bob)—to the United States in 1931. The boys were refused admission upon landing in August 1931; after two months, their father was called in and questioned at length. The inspectors seemed to doubt that the two were twins. They thought the boys were Doo Set's nephews or his grandsons, not his own children. They took statements from the boys' two older brothers, Ben and Bill, now eighteen and sixteen, who had also returned to the United States on the same steamer but who were not detained.[54] There were many discrepancies in the testimonies of the twins, their older brothers, and Wong Doo Set. Ironically, the family may not have studied the true facts of their case as well as they would have if they had been seeking to prove a "paper son" connection. However, Doo Set appealed their case within the requisite one week with a photo taken of the family three years earlier. Incredibly, the very distinct eyebrows of Wong Mun Soo (Uncle Bob) were apparent in the photo taken when he was not quite a year old. Also present in the photo are Doo Set's wife, his daughter, daughter-in-law, and the older sons Ben and Bill. The nine-year-old boys were ordered to be landed on October 28, 1931, after two months in detention on Angel Island.[55]

It is unknown what caused Doo Set to bring the twins at such a young age, but he may have wished them to attend school in Beloit like their older brothers, Ben and Bill. However, when Doo Set asked Charles and Yee Shee to take the boys, they refused. In late fall 1931 business at the restaurant was down, and their house in Beloit was already bursting at the seams with their own four children and the two older boys. So the twins moved to Chicago and lived with their father, who was in his late fifties. They attended Haines

Wong Doo Set's family in China in 1922: Mun Nging (Bill), daughter-in-law Yee Shee Gok, Lai Fong, wife Yee Shee (with Mun Soo and Mun Tai), and Mun Bin (Ben). (30734/3–23 WONG Ben Yuk file, NARA San Bruno)

School at 23rd and Wentworth, in Chicago, and NARA documents state that Doo Set's medical practice was at 146 W. 22nd Street, in Chinatown.[56] Tragically, in March 1934 Tai was killed by a streetcar.[57]

Doo Set would not live to practice in his home office in the village in his old age. Sick with a kidney infection, he was heading home to China in 1934 when he was admitted to the Chinese Hospital in San Francisco. He died there on April 29, 1934, at age sixty.[58] After his death, Doo Set's sons, Ben, Bill, and Bob, ages twenty-one, nineteen, and thirteen, accompanied his body back to China. Family from as far away as Hong Kong returned to Mong Dee for the burial.[59] Wong Doo Set's body rests at the cemetery on Dai Hill, which overlooks the New Village of Mong Dee.[60]

Having resolved the question of Wong Doo Set's identity and why he did not sponsor his oldest son, Charles Wong, we now examine the immigration and unfolding of Charles Wong's story.

CHAPTER TWO

Immigration and Settlement in Beloit

Charles Wong

As a boy of seventeen, Wong Theong (Charles Wong) left China to join relatives in the United States.[1] He left China in 1909 to join his uncle Wong Chow and other relatives in the western United States three years before his father emigrated. Charles returned to Mong Dee to marry in 1913. In 1920 Charles and several male relatives opened a restaurant in a prosperous small industrial city in the Midwest—Beloit, Wisconsin. Although he initially may have intended to live separately from his wife, Yee Shee, and return periodically to China, he decided to bring her from China and raise his family in the United States. They built a life together in Beloit.

Charles Wong's immigration to the United States in 1909 fit the pattern of migration of other young men from Guangdong. The eldest son of herbal doctor Wong Doo Set, Charles was born in the home village of Mong Dee in October 1891. His mother died when he was a teen, leaving Charles and one sister motherless, but in a community of many relatives.[2] At age seventeen, Charles immigrated to the United States as the "paper son" of a man named Wong Soon Pon. He traveled with a "paper brother" named Wong Git, who was supposedly one year older. There is no record of the relationship between the Wong family and Wong Soon Pon, and it is unclear who exactly Wong Git was. The fact that their paper father said both sons were in *Ock Lung* (Wisconsin) in 1922 suggests Wong Git may have been a close family member.[3] In spite of not knowing those exact relationships, we do know that the person who vouched for Charles's identity as he entered the United States

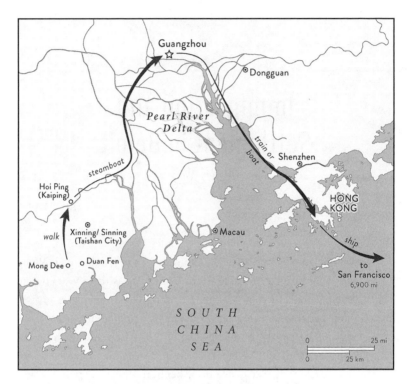

Voyage from Mong Dee to San Francisco, c. 1909. (Erin Greb Cartography)

was his uncle Wong Chow (a.k.a. Wong Doo Sung), his father's fourth brother, who was also from Mong Dee village.[4] Only ten years apart in age, the two men became very close over the years. Following the trajectory of other Chinese sojourners, Charles likely worked in a restaurant in Ogden, Utah, for three years in exchange for lodging and board.[5] After the three-year apprenticeship, his sponsor would have paid for his return trip to China so that the young man could marry and establish a home and family in his home village.

Charles and Yee Shee's 1913 Wedding in Mong Dee

Fulfilling one of the most significant life goals of a pious son, Charles returned to Mong Dee in October 1913 to marry Yee Shee.[6] According to Chinese Confucian tradition, marriage for both husband and wife marked the

Certificate of Identity of Wong Theong (a.k.a. Charles Wong), 1915. (WONG Theong file, NARA San Bruno)

beginning of their adult lives. Chinese men used their adult name for the first time at marriage, and they used that name for the rest of their lives.[7] Charles's father used his married name, "Wong Doo Set," for example, only after his marriage. His birth name would never again be used formally in China.

A photo commemorates Charles and Yee Shee's marriage on December 16, 1913. In the photo, they both wear traditional garb. Charles is dressed in a long, floral silk damask gown covered by a dark silk jacket with high collar and black knotted fasteners. Twenty years old, Yee Shee is in a two-piece dress, a white floral top with billowing sleeves, a red skirt, white stockings, and embroidered floral shoes. Their expressions reflect the seriousness of the occasion and perhaps the trepidation of embarking on a life with a partner they had not previously met.

For the couple and the family, the ceremony was a happy event attended by many guests.[8] A typical wedding ceremony in this region and era lasted three days, but the preparations for the event lasted longer.[9] An elderly "good luck" lady would have trimmed the hair on Yee Shee's forehead and pulled two red threads across the forehead to open (*hoi min*) her face into the square shape visible in the photograph. This practice, an indication that a young woman was married, invoked a blessing that the new bride would bear many sons. This was the final act of the bride's month-long period of isolation in a small room before the wedding. During that time, her unmarried girlfriends brought food, combed her hair, and kept her company. They

Wedding portrait of Yee
Shee Gok and Charles
Wong, 1913. (David Palmer)

sang "bridal laments" about the changes the bride would face after marriage.
The friends also went out to gather sticky plants (*chee tau mong*) that would
adhere to the clothes and hair of members of the wedding procession. On
the final day in her village, Yee Shee visited the ancestral hall in her parents'
village to pay respects and bid them farewell. She would hereafter be part of
the Wong family.

Because Yee Shee was Charles's first wife, the ceremony involved a red
bridal sedan chair (*tai hung fa kui*), a large, patterned umbrella (*tai long san*),
and the use of cloth that was embroidered with symbols of happiness (*hei
cheung*). Yee Shee dressed in her ceremonial clothes at her parents' home,
climbed into the sedan chair, and was carried by four bearers to Mong Dee
village.

Multiple wedding banquets for relatives and friends commemorated the
marriage over the three days. Each banquet had a specific purpose. On the first
day, the banquet welcomed the bride's dowry—the gifts her family provided

for the couple and for the groom's parents. The bride's family provided every-thing Yee Shee would need in her new home: furniture, crockery, kitchen utensils, bedding, and her own clothing and jewelry.[10] The banquet on the second day celebrated the wedding itself. It was customary for the guests to tease the bride during the wedding banquet. This would test her tempera-ment: Could she take a joke or not? They might tease her or goad her to sip alcohol, sing a song, or recite poetry. Two events took place on the third day: a tea ceremony and a return to Yee Shee's village. A ritual tea ceremony (*ching chi*) was offered to the elder relatives in the Wong family's ancestral hall in Mong Dee, the building that Charles's father, Wong Doo Set, later described with such pride.[11] The elders dressed in silk damask gowns with auspicious emblems sewn into the fabric. A middleman called out each of Charles's elder relatives by name, sitting them down in order of seniority in the center of the hall. Yee Shee offered them tea; in return they offered her a red packet (*laisee*) with money, jewelry, or possibly gold. That same day, Charles and Yee Shee returned to her parents' village and served a roasted pig that was provided by the Wong family. After their marriage, Charles re-mained in China for a year and a half. An extended stay would have allowed the couple to set up house in Mong Dee and start a family, though the two had no known surviving children from this period.

Charles and Yee Shee likely intended to repeat the marriage pattern so many of their relatives experienced, with Charles returning overseas to work, leaving Yee Shee in the village with her mother-in-law and the extended Wong clan. Charles departed China in 1915 and would not return for eight years. As he reentered the United States in 1915, Charles claimed a son the family knows no further information about, either because the child died (and their parents never shared the sadness with the children) or to establish an immigration slot they could later give, trade, or sell to family members or others. In 1915 Charles returned to Ogden, Utah, for an unknown period of time before moving first to San Francisco and then to the Midwest.[12]

If it is unclear why Charles went to California, he had a very good reason to leave. In 1916 he had a frightening interaction with U.S. immigration at his job in San Francisco. He was working as a cook in the household of Julian J. Meyer, a young investment banker in San Francisco.[13] On a mission to detect fraud in an immigrant brother's case, immigration agents dropped in on twenty-four-year-old Charles at his employer's home and interviewed him about his alleged brother and alleged father. The household itself was in disarray because the Meyer family was preparing to move. Charles, who had been working there for only a few months, told immigration officials that he would be out of work in three or four days. The paper sons phenomenon had, by that time, produced thousands of near-perfect interviews concerning immigrants' whereabouts, family connections, and descriptions of home villages in China. Thus agents were surprised that Charles's interview was so weak. He did not remember, for example, what date in the previous year his alleged son had been born. He remembered brothers' names, but

Map of the United States showing Beloit, Wisconsin. (Erin Greb Cartography)

not their dates of birth (absolutely required in interviews for which immigrants prepared). He no longer knew the name of his mother's village. He could not remember whether his alleged grandmother was alive in 1915 when he returned to the United States or whether his grandmother had natural or bound feet. To Charles's relief, Mrs. Meyer interrupted the interview and demanded it be concluded as quickly as possible so he could get back to work. Although they left shortly afterward, this interview caused agents to question the legality of Charles's claim to citizenship.[14] It also spurred his move from the area.

Beloit, Wisconsin, as a Midwestern Industrial City

Charles joined Wong Chow, his uncle and good friend, as part owner of the Nan King Lo Restaurant in Beloit, Wisconsin.[15] The restaurant had been opened by two men named Wong during the economic boom that accompanied an industrial boom in the town during World War I.[16] Beloit is located on the Rock River and has access to the Mississippi River and a steady supply of fresh water and wood, all of which made it attractive as a manufacturing center as the Midwest developed between the 1850s and 1880s. The city had experienced rapid growth in the era of British-sponsored globalization between 1896 and 1914, and global integration of its main industrial businesses was accomplished prior to World War I.[17] Elements of that global integration included international sales, investments, and migration. The two largest firms—which would provide employment to the next generation of Wongs—were a papermaking-machine factory, Beloit Iron Works (later Beloit Corporation), and an engine manufacturer, Fairbanks, Morse and Company. Beloit Iron Works had made its first international contacts at the Chicago Columbian Exposition in 1893 and then sold papermaking machines all over the world, including four to China—two in 1897 and two in 1900. Other large industries in Beloit included Berlin Machine Works, Warner Instrument, and Freeman Shoes. Berlin Machine Works, which manufactured machines to process lumber, established offices and factories abroad early in the twentieth century. These industries required labor.

Migrants from overseas and from the U.S. South enabled the city to grow and prosper in the early decades of the twentieth century. In addition to being a strong base for international exports and manufacturing, Beloit attracted a diverse group of workers from the global labor force of the pre–World War I economy. Immigrants made up more than 10 percent of Beloit's population for decades, and they accounted for a larger percentage of new-comers. The city's population grew steadily between 1870 and 1920, a period in which 26 million persons immigrated to the United States overall. In 1900 Beloit showed a 65 percent population growth over 1890, much larger than the 22 percent national growth and 21 percent growth for the State of Wisconsin.[18] This growth trend continued in 1910 and 1920 when Beloit's population reached 22,568.

The immigrants that settled in Beloit were from the same groups that settled other towns and cities in the Midwest, such as Chicago and Milwaukee. Notably, millions of Germans and Irish came to the Midwest in the mid-nineteenth century. The largest number of Beloiters in the 1910 census traced their parents' nativity to Germany, Ireland, and Norway. Immigrant patterns changed in the period of new immigration between 1880 and 1924. As the Industrial Revolution impacted economies in southern and eastern Europe, immigrants from those nations arrived in much greater numbers. Industrial cities like Beloit attracted young men from these nations, and by 1910, Italians and Greeks seeking industrial jobs made up the largest number of immigrants arriving in Beloit.[19] At Fairbanks, Morse and Company in 1923, the number of workers born in Italy and Greece exceeded those born in Norway, Ireland, and Germany.[20] To attract and keep workers, the town also provided "integration services" to the immigrant population, including workforce education classes and English language and literacy classes. In 1915, for example, one night school class in basic literacy comprised six Italians, three Austrians, two Greeks, one Russian, and one Lithuanian.[21]

Another migrant group critical to Beloit's industrial development were African Americans from the U.S. South. This migration started as European migration slowed due to disruptions in transatlantic shipping during World War I. As Isabel Wilkerson argues in *The Warmth of Other Suns: The Epic Story of America's Great Migration*, Black migrants attracted by jobs in northern cities fled the rigid caste system. One of Wilkerson's protagonists, Ida Mae Brandon Gladney, left Okalona, Mississippi, in 1937 to join "half" of her in-laws in Chicago and Beloit.[22] In 1923 the number of Black workers at Fairbanks, Morse and Company exceeded the number of any other national group. Thus, the town Charles moved to was made up of many other first- and second-generation migrants and immigrants.

Although racial segregation existed in some cities for Chinese Americans, Charles Wong purchased a home in a mixed-race, mixed-ethnic neighborhood on the west side of the Rock River in Beloit. Segregation of neighborhoods by race and ethnicity did occur in Beloit, but it was less pronounced than in other midwestern industrial cities. Larger midwestern cities like Chicago, Milwaukee, and St. Louis had Little Italies and Black Belts. As seen in chapter 1, Chicago landlords had raised housing costs in one district, causing Chinese to move en masse to the area that became known as Chinatown. In Beloit, housing segregation by race occurred initially by industrial policy and later by real estate agents, but it does not seem to have affected Charles Wong's purchase of the family home at 1015 Lincoln Street.[23] Charles bought the property for one dollar "and other good and valuable considerations" from Norwegian immigrants Ole J. and Anna Olson.[24] There was a general east-west divide in the town. Located on the east side of the river, Fairbanks, Morse and Company built housing for white workers immediately to the east of the factory and housing for Black workers across the Rock River from the plant, on the west side. A history of the city marked this as "the only known company-built segregated facilities for Black workers."[25] And later in the twentieth century, Black Beloiters spoke of being discouraged by real estate agents from buying in particular neighborhoods. Immigrants could be found throughout the city. Italian families crowded into dwellings on Riverside near St. Paul's Catholic Church, built in 1914.

Nan King Lo Restaurant in the 1920s and 1930s

Industrial growth affected all sectors of the city's economy, including housing, retail shopping, banking, hotels, and restaurants.[26] In 1902 the State Statistical Bureau reported that Beloit industries offered the highest per capita wages in the State of Wisconsin.[27] The town's high wages allowed workers and middle-class elite alike to eat out. Historian Katherine Leonard Turner has examined the explosion in restaurants that served working-class and middle-class patrons alike starting in the 1880s but accelerating between 1900 and 1920.[28] In 1920 there were many more restaurants in Beloit than there had been in 1910.

As a dedicated business owner and family man, Charles Wong achieved much in the 1920s. By then, the Beloit Chinese community consisted mostly of the extended family of Wongs; as Charles and Yee Shee's family grew, they made up most of the Chinese people in town. Others were their cousins, some co-owners of the restaurant and other workers, all either single men or men whose families lived in China. Two Chinese businesses in adjacent buildings—the restaurant and a Chinese laundry—shared a backyard and men's living quarters. A Chinese man had purchased Coates Steam Laundry on Bridge Street in the first decade of the twentieth century, renamed it Wa Sam, and moved it to a location on the west side of the river near the corner of 3rd Street and West Grand. The building had previously been the pattern shop and storage for J. Thompson & Sons Manufacturing, a plow works operated by a Norwegian immigrant family.[29] Wa Sam laundry operated out of the first-floor storefront on 3rd Street with living quarters for workers on the second floor.[30] In 1914 two men named Wong opened the Lo Nanking Restaurant on West Grand and used the upstairs of the laundry as living quarters. Charles Wong may have moved to Beloit immediately when he left California in 1916, but he may also have lived in Chicago for a couple of years prior to moving to Beloit. We do know, however, that Charles and his close relatives owned the restaurant still known as Lo Nanking (and later called Nan King Lo and the Chop House) by 1920 and he lived in the workers' quarters with his uncle and two cousins until he returned to China to bring his wife, Yee Shee, back to Beloit in 1923.

Charles was temperamentally suited to owning and operating a business. Though not outgoing by nature, he cultivated a gregarious public persona. As the "front man," he needed to welcome customers to the restaurant and make them feel at home. Charles maintained good relationships with several families among Beloit's powerful elite.[31] He handled banking and payments for the operation. Finally, as his uncles brought additional family members to work at and learn the business, Charles trained and intervened in disputes among some of his younger relatives. He once had to

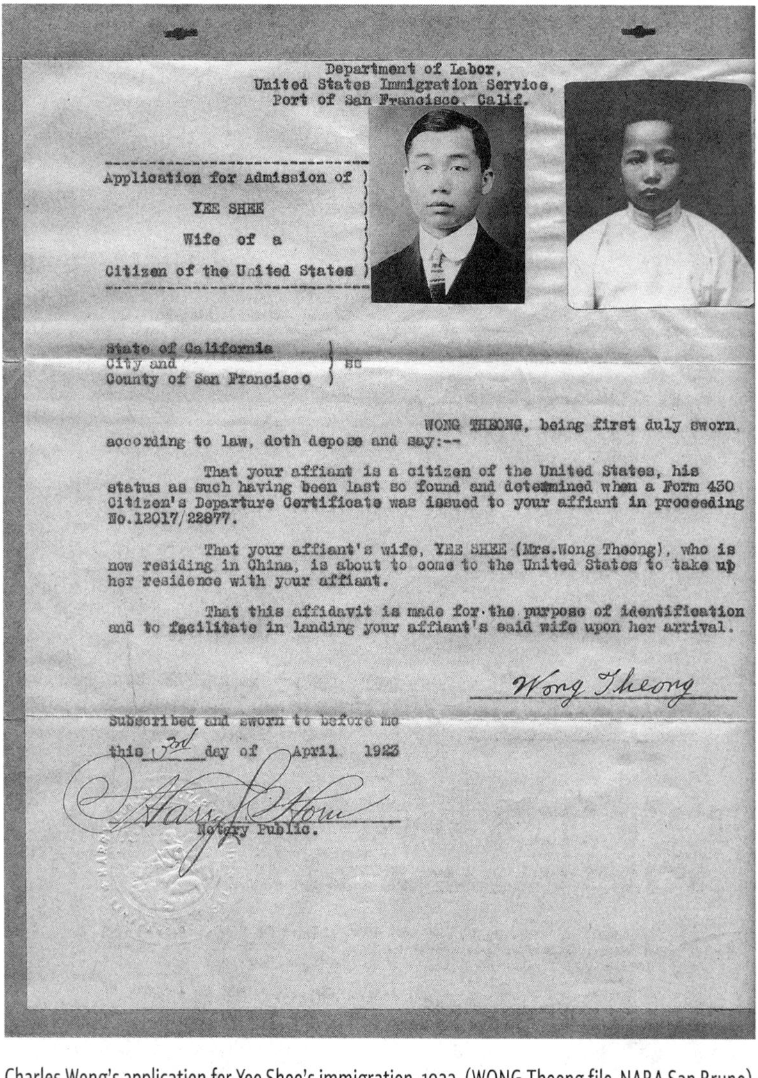

Department of Labor,
United States Immigration Service,
Port of San Francisco, Calif.

Application for Admission of)
)
YEE SHEE)
)
Wife of a)
)
Citizen of the United States)

State of California)
City and) ss
County of San Francisco)

WONG THEONG, being first duly sworn,
according to law, doth depose and say:--

That your affiant is a citizen of the United States, his
status as such having been last so found and determined when a Form 430
Citizen's Departure Certificate was issued to your affiant in proceeding
No.12017/22877.

That your affiant's wife, YEE SHEE (Mrs.Wong Theong), who is
now residing in China, is about to come to the United States to take up
her residence with your affiant.

That this affidavit is made for the purpose of identification
and to facilitate in landing your affiant's said wife upon her arrival.

Wong Theong

Subscribed and sworn to before me
this 3rd day of April 1923

Mary L Horn
Notary Public.

Charles Wong's application for Yee Shee's immigration, 1923. (WONG Theong file, NARA San Bruno) intervene in a fight between his half-brother, Ben, and a bad-tempered cousin, Don Wong.

Charles's children remember him as hardworking and loving, but stern. He worked seven days a week, leaving home in the late morning, coming back from about 2 to 4 in the afternoon, and returning home after midnight. He drove his black Ford automobile the three-quarters of a mile between the

Charles Wong's photo hung in the living room at 1015 Lincoln, c. 1930. (David Palmer)

Charles Wong heading to work in his car, 1930s. (Fung Scholz)

restaurant and home. Oldest son Gim remembered Charles starting the Model T on wintry mornings: "I used to go out in the morning with him and watch him start the Model T, jack up the front wheel, and then jack up the back wheel, pour a tea kettle of hot water over the block and get around and crank and crank it."[32] Charles did not spend a lot of time with his children, though George remembered going to the restaurant for French fried potatoes and, on Sundays, going for a ride in the family car.[33] His son Harry remembers going for rides in the countryside or going for ice cream with his dad. Charles's eldest daughter, Fung, who was twelve years old when he died, has many fond memories of him. On weekends or summer days, Fung used to walk over to the restaurant and catch a ride back with Charles when he came home for lunch. She also recalls watching him shave with a straight razor.

> The funniest thing was he'd get up and get dressed and come downstairs, and we had a big mirror in the cupboard in the kitchen, can you imagine? He'd stand there and shave with a straight razor, and he'd have a leather strap . . . and I would stand there watching him wondering why he didn't cut himself. He used to say, "What are you watching me for?" I'd say, "I just can't believe you don't cut yourself. You know, that takes practice." And I can remember him getting ready, and then he would say something to my mother about whether she needed anything before [he returned], cause she never went anyplace, ya know, he worked all the time. That's the only time I remember him being home, ten o'clock in the morning, about two to four . . . I'd never see him otherwise so he must have worked seven days a week.[34]

Charles took steps to assimilate his children into the Beloit community. Neither Charles nor Yee Shee were Christian or attended church. But Fung remembers that her father dressed her brother, Gim, and her in their best clothes and their single pair of shoes and walked them over to the West Side Presbyterian Church, on the corner of Liberty and 11th Street, several blocks from the house. There Charles introduced them to Pastor C. C. White and told him he wanted his children to have a religious education.[35] Their daughter Mary opines, "Perhaps this was [Father's] vision of making his children more American; I don't know what that was. [But] as a child, I remember

going to church and this whole community of church people welcoming us."
Ninety years later, several family members still attend the church.[36]

Charles could also deliver a stern rebuke. Fung remembers an incident
when, as a very young girl, she visited the men's quarters adjacent to the
restaurant above the Chinese laundry. Because both the restaurant and the
living quarters were on the second floor, wooden planks had been laid out
between the second stories of the buildings, which allowed the workers to
cross back and forth between them. Money must have been kept in the living
quarters because Charles sometimes crossed between the structures while
he was at work to pick up additional cash for the business. When Fung was
just a young girl, she once followed him across the planks to the men's quarters. She reported that the room was "disheveled," with unmade beds and
clothes everywhere on the floor. Her father admonished her, "You get back;
it's filthy over here."[37]

Evidence suggests the Beloit restaurant was very successful in the decade
of the 1920s. In addition to ownership in the restaurant, Charles and his
uncle, Wong Chow, who were best friends, saved money to purchase property together in Hong Kong, where they hoped to one day retire.[38] By the
1930s, especially after the Japanese invasion of China beginning in 1931, the
men realized that there was no future in their native village.[39] They purchased
five properties on Hennessy Road and on Egg Street in Hong Kong in the
1930s.[40] Each of the buildings had a business or store on the ground floor and
several floors of living space upstairs. Wong Chow later lived on-site and
managed the properties. Charles would not live to retire in Hong Kong.

On the night of July 15, 1938, a family dispute caused his cousin, Don
Wong, to shoot and kill Charles.[41] After midnight that Friday night at work,
the two got into an argument. Don ran across the planks to the living quarters to retrieve his 32-caliber revolver. He came back to the restaurant and
shot his cousin five times.[42] By that time, Don had been living in Beloit for
nine years, although his wife and children still lived in China.[43] Cousin Att
Wong called the police immediately, and they arrested Don and charged him
with premeditated murder. Don reportedly told the arresting officer, "Charley has been making trouble for me for a couple of months."[44] Charles was
rushed to Beloit Hospital but died before he got to an operating room.

Without records from either Charles or Don themselves, it is impossible to know whether the argument was personal or about business. There are reasons for both. As the eldest son of an eldest son, Charles had more status than Don did. He was a part owner of the restaurant, and Don was not. Additionally, Don was known to have had a gambling habit, and he may have asked to borrow money from the till to cover his debts. He also had a terrible temper. The local newspaper reported that Don had recently sparred with Charles's half-brother, Ben Wong, using kitchen knives, and that Charles had acted as the peacemaker in that fight.[45] Most likely there was a simmering dispute over Don's behavior, whether his gambling or his anger, that Charles had tried to quell.

Don Wong avoided a long prison sentence by claiming insanity. The early police report indicated that Don admitted guilt immediately, and when asked why he shot his cousin, he said, "I must have been crazy." In news reports in the Wisconsin press the day after the murder, other associates in the restaurant reported that Don had been ill.[46] Don pled guilty in the circuit court in nearby Janesville to the second-degree murder charge on November 22 of the same year, and he was sentenced to fourteen to twenty years in the state penitentiary at Waupun, in the Central State Hospital for the Insane.[47] Seventeen months later, in 1940, he was listed in the census among one hundred men, ages eighteen to eighty-three, at the facility.[48]

Charles's death had long-lasting consequences for his widow and children. Yee Shee had to determine whether to stay in Beloit or move to the family's other property in Hong Kong. Charles's proprietary share in the restaurant continued, and his son Gim took it over. In the very short run, Yee Shee was consumed by grief. The community in Beloit came forth with assistance.

CHAPTER THREE

Surviving and Thriving in Beloit

Yee Shee Wong

If not the most important Wong, Yee Shee is certainly the most heroic in the way she exceeded expectations and overcame the obstacles in her life. She surpassed the expectations for a Chinese woman born in the late nineteenth century, even while she conserved and passed along deeply held values to her children, adapting them as needed to meet her own and her family's needs. When her husband died unexpectedly, she managed to raise her children almost single-handedly, despite a very low income, and she saw them grow into productive adults who enjoyed good marriages and families of their own.

Yee Shee Gok was born on December 23, 1894, in Shitou village in Taishan county, Guangdong. She was the younger daughter and the fourth of five children of Yee Thien Wu and Liu Moi Han.[1] Yee Shee grew up in the first decade of the twentieth century, a time in the history of Confucian tradition when the family, according to Chinese philosopher Chen Lai, still formed the "social foundation" of Chinese family life.[2] Yee Shee trusted her parents and the matchmaker they engaged to select her husband. She later trusted her husband when he suggested she leave his village and join him in the United States.[3] With a houseful of their own children and two young half-brothers, they persevered through the Great Depression. After Charles's death, Yee Shee continued to raise and care for her young children even while managing her own grief; she drew on connections she had cultivated in her community. She encouraged the children to help each other. With her values buoyed by courage and strength of spirit, Yee Shee gave birth to and raised her children under immensely trying circumstances.

Although exactly what Confucianism meant was in flux as she came of age, many of Yee Shee's values reflected aspects of Confucian virtues.[4] Primary among these was a devotion to male relatives before, during, and after marriage; this included devotion to one's father before marriage, to one's husband during marriage, and to one's eldest son in widowhood. The most self-abnegating virtue was that daughters were of less value than sons.[5] A daughter was raised to marry well and bring value to her in-laws' household. Because a good marriage depended on finding a young man who was educated or wealthy, Yee Shee's parents were likely attracted to Charles Wong because of the family's reputation and the prosperity they generated from work overseas. In turn, Charles's parents were likely attracted to Yee Shee because of her health, her homemaking skills, and her potential to be a good mother to their future grandsons.

Yee Shee was an asset to the marriage by health, temperament, and training.[6] A photo of Yee Shee taken around the time of Charles and Yee Shee's

Yee Shee Gok, 1923. (WONG Theong file, NARA San Bruno)

wedding in 1913 shows her in a photo studio with her mother and two sisters-in-law. All four women were wearing pants and tunics with slippers and appeared to be healthy, calm, and beautiful.[7] Yee Shee's mother, who was about fifty years old in the photo, looked young and dynamic.[8] In keeping with trends in young girls' education in Guangdong at the time, Yee Shee had been only minimally educated prior to her marriage, but she had excellent domestic skills, especially when it came to sewing and embroidery. Her family was relatively well-off—possibly the wealthiest family in their village—but likely not among the Westernized elite of that era, who typically sent their daughters off to missionary boarding schools at about age seven.

Yee Shee produced no heirs during the time that she lived in Mong Dee village, though she suffered losses that may have included a child and miscarriages.[9] Her father died three months after Yee Shee and Charles were married, likely prompting an extended stay back home.[10] Even so, she lived with Charles in Mong Dee village for more than a year and, in spite of that relatively lengthy time together, they had no children before they came to the United States. Like other Chinese wives, Yee Shee's duties in Mong Dee

Yee Shee Gok with her mother and sisters-in-law, 1913. (David Palmer)

were determined by her mother-in-law, Doo Set's second wife. Among those duties was the expectation that she would help care for her husband's step-brothers, Ben and Bill, and also Bob and Tai, the twins who were born the year she departed.[11]

Yee Shee distinguished herself among Chinese women of her station by becoming literate. Young women who studied in China in the first decades of the twentieth century might have had a tutor come to their house or they might have attended a local school for girls. There is no record of either of these for Yee Shee, although the fact that she learned Chinese writing later in life suggests that she was at least tutored, even if she did not attend primary school for the customary three years. It was after her marriage, while she was living in Mong Dee, that Wong Chow—Charles's uncle, friend, and business partner in both the restaurant in Beloit and in the properties held in Hong Kong—urged Yee Shee to study Chinese. That way she could keep in touch with her family members in China by international mail. Her daughter, Mary, distinctly remembers addressing airmail letters to relatives in Hong Kong because Yee Shee had never learned to read or write in English, except to sign her name.

A Chinese Woman Immigrant to the United States in the Era of Exclusion

Yee Shee came to the United States with Charles after he joined his uncles in opening a restaurant business there. Soon after their arrival, Charles purchased a home on the west side of Beloit. By the very act of coming to the United States and then settling in a small Midwest town, Yee Shee surpassed the expectations for Chinese women of her generation. Chinese custom and American laws worked together to keep most Chinese women at home in China. On the Chinese side, most men intended to be sojourners, to earn money abroad but maintain a family in their home villages where their children would continue their family lines, remaining close to and venerating their ancestors. Sojourners would return home to make sure that their families were doing well and to engage in marital visits that would ensure additional children. With so many Chinese men living alone in the United States, however, a sex trade thrived there.[12] Because of the rampant stereotyping of

Chinese women as prostitutes, U.S. immigration officials were concerned about any young Chinese woman who entered the United States, married or not.[13] The Page Act of 1875, which sought to prohibit the entry of unfree laborers and women brought for "immoral purposes," was enforced primarily against Chinese women.

The issue of U.S. immigration officials' suspicion of Chinese women had a class element as well, which played out with peculiar outcomes. Women from elite Chinese families had practiced foot-binding during the Qing and prior dynasties. Starting in girlhood, a girl's feet would be bound so tightly that the bindings would eventually break the arch and bend the toes under, keeping the foot quite small and, when wearing shoes, dainty looking. Many Chinese appreciated the erotic appeal of these small feet and the delicate gait they produced.[14] Scholar and poet Wang Ping explored how foot-binding became quite widespread during the Song and Qing Dynasties. Early on foot-binding was a symbol of the leisure classes and their ideals of femininity. But during the foreign dynasties, when the Han were invaded and ruled by the Manchu, foot-binding went from a practice of excess "cultural and economic consumption" to become an expression of Han identity and "the safeguard of (Chinese) morality."[15] As China modernized in the late Qing and early Republican era, Chinese leaders linked women's health to the health of the nation, declaring that foot-binding should be ended and women should be educated.[16]

Ironically, U.S. immigration officials thought that this custom was of practical value in determining the class status of a Chinese woman. Since only elite families could afford to have a woman's working ability damaged by walking on broken feet, and since, after 1882, elites were exempt from the rules prohibiting the immigration of Chinese to the United States, American immigration officials assumed Chinese women with bound feet were of the elite class and therefore admissible as visitors or immigrants. In contrast, women with unbound feet were closely scrutinized and sometimes deported on the suspicion that they were prostitutes. Yee Shee had unbound feet. She told her daughter and granddaughter that her family had started the process of foot-binding with her, but she had asked that it be discontinued because it hurt so much.[17] As the wife of a U.S. citizen, Yee Shee should have been granted easy admittance to the United States, but as previously noted, Chinese Americans were very often denied even the most entrenched rights when it came to immigration practices. Whether her family was more modern or less elite, the fact that Yee Shee did *not* have bound feet presented a problem for Charles when it came to bringing her to the United States. He resolved the problem by purchasing first-class tickets for their travel, thereby marking the two of them as elite and making it far less likely that her right to enter—or her morality—would be challenged.

Charles needed to act quickly to bring Yee Shee to the United States in 1923 for two reasons. First, the political situation in Guangdong was extremely unstable. The Kuomintang, the Chinese Nationalist Party, had made an alliance with the regional warlord, Chen Jiongming, who had established military control over the area. When Nationalist leader Sun Yat-Sen suggested to Chen that they combine forces and send an expeditionary force to overthrow the warlord in Beijing, Chen declined and rose in rebellion against Sun. The two sides fought ferociously—with other warlords also joining the fight—and it took until January 1923 to establish peace in the province. A second reason was that Chinese Americans had become aware that the U.S. Congress was planning to again tighten immigration laws. One provision in the immigration law under consideration by Congress in 1923 would permanently exclude wives of U.S. citizens "who were ineligible to naturalize," in other words, wives of Asian Americans like Charles.[18] If Charles was going to bring Yee Shee to the United States at all, he needed to act immediately.

In the summer of 1923 Charles and Yee Shee crossed the Pacific Ocean as first-class passengers aboard the SS *President McKinley*, and Yee Shee entered Seattle easily and without detention. The trip must have been exhilarating for the couple, though surely also tainted by worries about the reception they might face on the U.S. side. Departing Hong Kong on August 2, the ship stopped in Shanghai; Kobe, Japan; Yokohama, Japan; and Victoria, British Columbia before it arrived in Seattle two and a half weeks later. Many passengers experienced intense seasickness during the voyage, and being three months pregnant (with eldest son, Gim) likely exacerbated that experience for Yee Shee. Yee Shee was, moreover, one of only four women and girls among thirty-two Chinese passengers on the ship.[19] But the first-class ticket strategy

Admiral Oriental Line brochure, 1923. (WFP, Beloit College Archives)

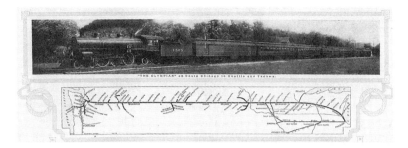

Train route from Seattle to Chicago in 1923. (Washington State University)

worked, and Yee Shee entered the United States easily. In Seattle, Charles and Yee Shee recuperated from the voyage for a few days at a rooming house at 701 King Street before taking a train across the country. Although no documentation remains of the trip, they likely booked a sleeper car on the *Olympian* operated by the Chicago, Milwaukee, and St. Paul Railway, all the way from Seattle to Beloit, a trip that would have taken three days.[20]

Racial Stratification in 1920s Beloit

In Beloit, Wisconsin, in the early 1920s, Yee Shee and Charles negotiated a racist society stratified by social class, although being among the few Chinese in a town that had become accustomed to Chinese students at the nearby college lessened the expression of anti-Chinese racism. Racism against African Americans grew in the northern states in the 1920s.[21] Articles about race in the *Beloit Daily News* ranged from the trivial to the detrimental. Race had been of great interest to Beloit newspaper readers since 1914, when Black laborers began to migrate from the South, particularly from Mississippi, to replace European laborers whose immigration was prevented by the outbreak of World War I. The census showed a change in the Black population in Beloit from fewer than one hundred persons in 1910 to nearly one thousand in 1920, which was about 4 percent of the total population.[22] In 1923 the *Beloit Daily News* ran an article about the (albeit spurious) research of a Yale University professor who had attended Beloit College as an undergraduate. He argued that having colored skin displaced energy that would be used for work and advancement.[23] Although the researcher generalized his results, there is little evidence of negative information about non-Black people of color in Beloit.

Ads in the *Beloit Daily News* showed racialized images of Black and Asian peoples, but the number of ads and derisiveness of the images indicated that racialization of Black people was harsher. An archival search found few depictions of Asians in ads or cartoons. There was an ad for a shoe polish in 1915 that depicted stylized images of a white, a Black, and an Asian boy, for white, black, and tan shoe polish. Another ad for a product called "Chi-namel" used a stylized image of an Asian baby. Finally, a drawing of a beautiful Asian woman departing the bath was used to sell "Jap Rose" soap, which "leaves the skin soft and perfectly clean." These ads suggest racialization and othering based on skin color, as well as the sexualization of Asian women, but they nevertheless stand in contrast to the highly offensive ads depicting African Americans in more derisive ways.[24]

In its news articles of the same period, the *Beloit Daily News* sympathetically covered changing mores and rising ecumenicalism among Chinese Christians.[25] In the 1910s and 1920s Christian missionaries in China, whether Westerners or, increasingly, Western-educated Chinese students who returned to China as missionaries, began to encourage Chinese Christians to include elements of Chinese tradition in their Christian practice. Beloit College began training young Chinese Christians in 1914.[26] The college benefited from the application of an indemnity forced on the Chinese government by the Western powers after the Boxer Rebellion, which paid the tuition of Chinese studying to become ministers at American universities. In fact, Beloit College alum and well-known China missionary Arthur Henderson Smith proposed the idea of using the indemnity in this manner to President Theodore Roosevelt.[27] The number of Chinese students at the college grew after 1914, and the students actively promoted Chinese culture locally. On October 10, 1919, the Beloit Chinese Students Club hosted an event to celebrate the eighth anniversary of the Chinese Republic, drawing a crowd of three hundred "interested and sympathetic Beloiters."[28] It is possible that the Chinese restaurant that appeared in Beloit around the same time opened to accommodate the growing number of Chinese students at Beloit College.

More likely, word about industrial Beloit's growth and untapped restaurant market, and openness to Chinese people, circulated in Chicago's Chinese community.

In February 1921, two years before Yee Shee came to Beloit, the Chinese Students Club at Beloit College sponsored an event to celebrate Chinese culture and raise money for famine relief in China. Nearly five hundred people attended the event, which brought Chinese musicians from the University of Wisconsin in Madison to accompany two plays, *The Match of Gold and Jade* and *The World of Fools*. The students cleared almost $200 for famine relief at two shows in Beloit and Rockton.[29] As the Chinese community in Chicago had broadcast to their relatives on the West Coast decades earlier, overall there was less discrimination against Chinese in the Midwest than in the West.

Building Community in 1920s and 1930s Beloit

Once Yee Shee was settled in the house on Lincoln Avenue, the family experienced several joyous years. Charles's daily life vastly improved by having moved out of the all-male rooms behind the restaurant and into a house of his own with his wife. Charles worked seven days a week but returned home every afternoon for lunch and a nap on the fainting couch in the front hallway on the ground floor. During the first years after her arrival, Yee Shee gave birth to three children, Gim, Fung, and George, at Beloit Hospital. In addition to the blessings of those healthy births, their family grew in other ways. Charles's much younger half-brothers, Bin and Nging (Ben and Bill), arrived in 1925 and came to live not with their father, Doo Set, in Chicago, but with Yee Shee and Charles in Beloit. They knew Yee Shee from their early days of living with her in Mong Dee village.

As her family grew, the burden on Yee Shee must have been immense, for she had no mother, sister, or close friends to share her work, as she would have had in China. In a household of means in China, servants would have done much of the cooking, cleaning, and laundry, though girls and women of the household would have sewn and embroidered clothes and slippers. Her children remember Yee Shee as eminently capable and resourceful. In addition to cooking every meal and cleaning, she sewed, washed, ironed, and mended their clothes. She was also a prodigious gardener. She kept vegetable and

Charles, Yee Shee, and Gim Wong, 1924. (Fung Scholz)

BELOIT, WIS. Mch-6- 1926.

Mrs. Chas Wong

IN ACCOUNT WITH BELOIT HOSPITAL

Feb.	24	25 - Room 229ᵗ - 2days @ 5.00	10	00
"	"	maternity fee -	12	00
Feb.	25	mch. 6 - 8days @ 4.00	32	00
mch	4	gym .	1	00
			$55	00

Paid Beloit Hospital
March 6 - 1926

DOCTORS BILL NOT INCLUDED

Beloit Hospital bill for Fung Wong's birth, 1926. (Fung Scholz)

Ben, Yee Shee, Grandfather, Charles, Bill, Fung, and Gim Wong, 1928. (David Palmer)

flower gardens in the summer, and she instructed the children how to pick fruit from three cherry trees, a pear tree, and an apple tree in the backyard. The family practiced home economy, too, canning the fruit from the trees in the summertime. Frugality was the rule, yet even in times of want, the Wongs shared the bounties of their garden with neighbors.

Without close female relatives, Yee Shee cultivated relationships with their neighbors, many of whom were first- and second-generation immigrants. The neighborhood, with immigrants from Norway, Denmark, Sweden, Hungary, and Germany, was typical of Beloit's 10 percent immigrant population.[30] Though she spoke little English, Yee Shee interacted with and befriended her neighbors. Emma Antonsen, who lived on Merrill Street with her Swedish immigrant husband, Charles, and grown daughter, Margaret, taught Yee Shee to make an anise cookie that is a Wong family Christmas favorite to this day. A Jewish family, Moses and Cora Rosenblatt and their daughter, Fanchon, lived across the street. Moses, son of a merchant tailor who emigrated from Germany, had owned a factory in Beloit. At Christmastime, Yee Shee made a hot dinner of rice and a special chop suey out of the fattest and freshest, home-cultivated mung bean sprouts and homemade chow mein noodles.[31] She sent the children to deliver the meal to their neighbors. Home economy and good neighborly relations allowed the family to survive the trying times ahead.

Life in the United States during the 1930s was difficult for the Wongs, and they contemplated returning to China. The worldwide Great Depression impacted the local economy, causing thousands in Beloit to be laid off and affecting business at Nan King Lo restaurant. The wife of an owner of a similar restaurant in Indianapolis said about their business, "The restaurant used to make over two hundred dollars a day on lunch meals alone [catering to working men]. During the Depression we were lucky to make two or three dollars per day."[32] Unlike that restaurant, the Beloit restaurant managed to stay afloat. Yee Shee continued to have successful pregnancies, giving birth to Helen, Harry, and Frank in 1931, 1933, and 1935. Yet a photo from 1935, presumably taken by Charles, suggests family stress. The photo is of Yee Shee, who looks exhausted, with the six children. The snapshot is taken in front of one of the fruit trees in the backyard, in summer. Yee Shee and the girls (Fung and Helen) are in handmade dresses and Gim is in a short-sleeved button-down shirt; the smaller boys (George and Harry) are in handsewn playsuits; the baby (Frank) is in a T-shirt and diapers. The children's hair is neatly combed. All of the children but Gim are barefoot, and George seems to have been called in from playing because his playsuit is soiled. It is at this point that we must contemplate the distinct hardships of giving birth to and raising children in an uncertain economic climate without female relatives.

Beyond the effects of the Great Depression, Charles and Yee Shee had suffered a double loss in the year before this photo was taken. In 1931 Charles's father, Wong Doo Set, had brought his twin sons, Bob and Tai, to the United States, even though they were still quite young. Doo Set may have had in mind that they could be folded right into the Wong family in Beloit, with Yee Shee acting as their mother, as she did for Bin and Nging. But the couple

George, Fung, Yee Shee with Frank, Gim with Harry, Helen, 1935. (David Palmer)

already had four children plus at least one of the half-brothers, Nging, in their modest home in Beloit. Given this, as Yee Shee later told her children, she and Charles had to say "no" to her father-in-law, which went against her understanding of family obligations.[33] So the nine-year-old twins joined their father, then in his fifties, in Chicago's male-dominated Chinatown. They attended school in Chicago, but they may have lacked supervision. Early in 1934 eleven-year-old Tai was struck and killed by a streetcar in Chicago. The tragedy certainly weighed heavily on his father, who decided at that point to return to China with his three young sons. Doo Set fell sick, and his illness was exacerbated by the painful loss of his youngest son. It was en route back to China, in April 1934, that Doo Set died in San Francisco.

In the midst of the Depression and now that Charles's father no longer lived nearby, Charles and Yee Shee decided to leave the United States. In 1936, the year before baby Mary was born, the Wong family put their house on the market with the intent of returning to China. A small sign on the front porch advertised that the house was for sale and the older children remember attending going away parties that were given for them at school. But the house did not sell, and so the family remained in Beloit. At that point, Charles and Yee Shee had little choice but to persevere and continue to make sacrifices to give their children a better chance in America.

Surviving and Thriving in Beloit, Wisconsin:
Family and Community

After Charles Wong was shot and killed on July 16, 1938, the family overseas made an effort to encourage Yee Shee to bring the children to Hong Kong. By this time, her husband's uncle and close friend, Wong Chow, lived in Hong Kong full-time, and he offered to help raise the children. Yee Shee must have considered the offer seriously, but in the end she decided to stay in Beloit. She and Charles had immigrated to the United States to give their children a better life and more opportunities. Primary among the opportunities, according to Yee Shee's values, was that education is "the one thing

Gim, Fung, George, Helen, Harry, Frank, and Mary Wong, summer 1937. (David Palmer)

that can never be taken away."[34] However difficult it was for the family, the children should finish their educations here.

Her children were aware of the toll their father's death took on Yee Shee. Fung, George, and Harry reported that they heard their mother cry herself to sleep every night that summer, wailing so loud that the neighbors could also hear her—and the neighbors responded. One neighbor, Avis Bord, cared for Yee Shee's seventeen-month-old baby, Mary, for a period of time, perhaps as long as four months. Also a single mother, Avis had two older girls, ages ten and twelve, and two younger boys, ages seven and eight.[35] Mary's siblings remember that Yee Shee went to the Bords every day to visit her child. No doubt Mrs. Antonsen and her daughter Margaret also brought food and lent a hand. A local relief agency offered the family some help. At Christmastime, the Family Welfare Agency reached out to the Wongs and asked each of the children what they wanted for Christmas. Fung remembers asking for and receiving a doll.[36] In this way, the Wongs' neighbors and the community provided the immediate support the family needed to persevere after the tragic loss of their husband and father.

The children's financial help to their mother was essential to the family's survival over the following decades. Only fourteen years old when his father died, Gim did not wish to leave the restaurant staff, and so he continued to work at the restaurant for several months and rode his bicycle every morning to collect receipts and deposit them in the bank. It soon became clear that it would be impossible for him to work at the restaurant and keep up his high school studies. At that point, Yee Shee sold her share of the restaurant to her husband's cousin—the brother of Charles's murderer—after which she and the family "never set foot in the restaurant again."[37]

In contemplating her immediate future, Yee Shee had her house and the proceeds from the sale of her share in the restaurant. The house was paid off. Although she believed she was taken advantage of by men she did not trust, she accepted $1,500 for Charles's share of the restaurant on her own and her children's behalf, as settled by Western Title Company in 1939. Yee Shee opened bank accounts in each of the children's names and used the money in their accounts to purchase food in subsequent years.[38] The older children worked while they were still in high school, holding part-time jobs while school was in session and full-time in the summer, and they gave what money they earned to their mother. In a model expression of Chinese family values (which nonetheless exacted a toll), the older children sacrificed much to help their mother and younger siblings survive—and thrive.

Yee Shee's control over family-owned properties also helped her persist through the hard years with many children and no spousal support. Ten years after Charles's death she returned to Hong Kong in June of 1948 with Gim to sell two Hong Kong properties.[39] In Yee Shee's absence, Fung, who was working as a registered nurse in Madison, was called home to care for her younger siblings, the youngest of whom were in their early teens. Yee Shee and Gim sold a property on Hennessy Road and another on Egg Street in Hong Kong, keeping a half share of a final property on Hennessy Road until 1977 when the Crown Colony purchased it so that they could widen the road.[40] In the 1948 trip, Yee Shee reestablished family relations and made new connections in Hong Kong.[41] It was not possible to visit Mong Dee, so Yee Shee sent money for family, including Grandfather Wong Doo Set's second wife and a couple of cousins to come to Hong Kong to visit them.

Harry, Frank, Gim, George, Mary, Yee Shee, Helen, Fung Wong, 1950. (David Palmer)

On the way home, Gim and Yee Shee stopped in Shanghai, where they were reunited with Ben (Wong Mun Bin), the older of the two step-uncles who had lived with the family in Beloit for several years. At the time, Ben, who had learned to fly at the airport in Janesville, Wisconsin, was flying planes for the Chinese National Aviation Corporation.[42] The sale of the Hong Kong properties resulted in many gifts for the family back in Beloit. Yee Shee brought jade and opal jewelry for her daughters and jeweled watches for her sons. She even brought back bracelets, necklaces, and rings for her sons' future brides. Additionally, she brought silk tapestries, silk fabric, ivory elephants, and a set of carved wooden animals for each child.

Yee Shee continued to inculcate the children with Chinese values—and follow them herself—as they grew up. Her support involved remaining at home to care for them behind the scenes; several of her children said she "did not leave the house for nine years" after Charles died. This was in keeping with a Chinese virtue, as modeled by a woman named Boji (circa 580 BC) who chose not to leave her house even when it was engulfed by flames because of the moral code that a woman should not leave the house unchaperoned.[43] Nor was it acceptable, according to her upbringing, to try to remarry after Charles's death.[44] Yee Shee's task was to manage the household and raise the children. Another way that Yee Shee expressed her values was that she "concealed her sentiments" when it came to celebrating her children's achievements. Frank reported that when he told her he had received a national four-year scholarship that would allow him to attend Harvard University, she "glowed" for a moment and then sent him outside to "mow the lawn before it rained."[45] This value of modesty in the face of success is one that would be carried forward.

Yee Shee always had in mind that she, too, would repatriate to China one day, but after a trip to Hong Kong in 1957, she finally decided against it. Even though she felt accepted in the United States, she was Chinese and wanted to return. But her sister had traveled from the village to visit her in Hong Kong and told her how poorly elderly people with family abroad were treated in Communist China.[46] And her children and grandchildren were in the United States, and she needed to be where they were. After the U.S. repealed Chinese exclusion laws during World War II, Chinese citizens became eligible to naturalize. Yee Shee naturalized as an American citizen on November 9, 1959.[47] In the last decades of her life, she continued to live alone, but she would travel to visit her children and grandchildren. She was especially devoted to her grandchildren who, in turn, speak of her in reverent tones. They recall how she expressed her affection with food, catering to their tastes and making their favorite Chinese and American dishes.[48] She taught some of her grandchildren to prepare particular dishes, like eggrolls, that they cook to this day.[49] They remember, too, her quiet ways, her good disposition, and her cheerful manner.[50] As her daughter Mary put it, "She continued to nurture and be the model of a constant loving, supportive mother and grandmother to the end of her life."[51]

Yee Shee died of an aortic aneurysm at Beloit Hospital on December 1, 1978, at age eighty-three. The University of Wisconsin Extension in Janesville honored her as one of the "Inspirational Women—Past and Present." A further honor was bestowed by the Beloit Historical Society when it enshrined her in the Beloit Historical Hall of Fame in 1985. They did so based on her record as an outstanding mother and because she was the first Chinese

Portrait of Mother Wong, 1978.
(David Palmer)

woman to raise a family in Beloit. Her portrait and the award hang at the Historical Society's museum at the Lincoln Center in Beloit.

Considering the discriminatory federal laws against the Chinese over many years and the way she persevered in terrible conditions, Yee Shee Wong's story is heroic. She distinguished herself by telling her family she did not want her feet bound and by becoming literate in Chinese. Yee Shee was one of very few Chinese women to immigrate to the United States in the period of Chinese exclusion. Without close female relatives or a good command of the English language, she cultivated relationships with women neighbors in Beloit, sharing food and recipes through the Great Depression and beyond. Her strength continued in widowhood when she negotiated her husband's share of the family restaurant in Beloit and then followed her own counsel in her decision not to move her family back to China. To keep food on the table—helped out by children on the brink of adulthood—she sold shares of the family property in Hong Kong.

Yee Shee's legacy of raising and encouraging her children and grandchildren makes her an inspiration to her own family and to others. As her son Frank wrote in his eulogy to Mother Wong:

To her family, she had always been there, and it seemed she would always be there. Like some bountiful tree, she weathered the unpredictable storms of life with enduring resilience, always giving strength and nurture to those who came within the shelter of her protective limbs. So successfully had she overcome the extraordinary circumstances of her life, including outrageous misfortune, that to those close to her, time seemed to have no grip on her destiny. Yet she herself knew better, for even as she enjoyed her final years, she prepared for her departure, making sure that her affairs were in order, making sure that she would be giving to those she left behind, still the embodiment of mother's love, even in death as she was in life.

Now in her sudden absence, her presence remains a powerful force among us. She was not perfect in life; she had her human flaws, but now with her departure she is perfected in our memories. Her life, not her death, becomes a symbol that we carry with us. In one sense, Grandmother Wong has become Golden Chrysanthemum again, for to the Chinese there is an enduring meaning in that original name that was given to her. The chrysanthemum symbolizes strength and virtue, the one flower that survives the deathly frost of autumn. Gold symbolizes the universal value, the unchanging nature of that virtue. Although she accomplished most of her life in America, she did so with simple Chinese virtues that are also universal virtues; courage and compassion, strength and love, honesty and justice, all nourished by the extended roots of the family. Neither time nor death shall conquer these.

CHAPTER FOUR

Family, Work, and Wartime Service

Gim, Fung, and George Wong

The historical experiences of second-generation Chinese Americans were even more complicated than those of their immigrant parents' generation. Forming their identities during and after World War II, this generation received mixed messages about their fitness for citizenship. As children, they learned values at home in their immigrant families and in "one of the most important American socializing agents," the U.S. public school.[1] In a study of Chinese Americans who grew up on the West Coast, historian Sucheng Chan noted that while their teachers and peers accepted this generation as children, they experienced rejection from European American friends as adolescents.[2] Chinese American children's reactions to this discrimination ranged from repression to resistance to identification with China.

This study evidences the racism and othering the Wong children experienced before, during, and after the war. It compares the racism they experienced to that of second-generation Chinese American children on the West Coast and examines their identity formation. It shows that acculturation was well underway for the Wongs dating from their arrival in Beloit in 1923. The Wong children attended integrated schools where they excelled in academics and extracurriculars. They survived their father's death, thanks to the strength of their mother and their ties to the community. The story of the Wong family reflects both inner strength against racism and tragedy and a certain communal strength of their city in both the Depression and wartime economies.

The midwestern city of Beloit, Wisconsin, would experience its peak of growth and industrial production in 1955. The city had developed during a period of British-sponsored globalization prior to World War I, which allowed its major industries—Fairbanks, Morse and Company, Beloit Corporation, and Yates American, among others—to thrive during the war. After the 1930s slump, a second, much larger boost in wartime business sent production soaring. Both productive periods encouraged business integration with other facilities nationally and, in both periods, internationally. Yates American, for example, which produced machines that sanded wood, followed a downturn in wood processing in the Midwest by opening facilities in the West and especially in Canada during and after World War I. Fairbanks and Beloit Corporation had facilities across the industrial Great Lakes and overseas. Attending high school before and during the war, the older Wong children came of age in a booming local economy with corporations that sought industrial and managerial talent.

The siblings can be thought of in two groups, the older three and the younger four. The division is somewhat arbitrary, especially when considering the middle siblings, but in this account, the older children stayed closer to home, working and ensuring that their mother survived the death of her husband. They earned money to buy food and clothing for the family, and they laid a pathway for their younger siblings. Finishing high school between 1942 and 1946, the older three served in the U.S. Armed Forces, which helped them cobble together resources to attend college. All three had successful careers; all three chose white midwesterners as spouses and raised families mainly in the Midwest. Their experiences help us understand how second-generation Chinese Americans employed strong personal and familial values and overcame racism to succeed in institutions in an expanding economy and a changing American society.

Serving Family and Community: Gim

Gim Wong's position in the family demanded a lot of him. He was, after all, the oldest son of an oldest son (Charles) of an oldest son (Doo Set). Gim had been conceived in Mong Dee village and was born in Beloit; he spoke only Chinese until he started playing with other kids on the street.[3] As one of the oldest, Gim (and the next oldest, his sister, Fung) faced more racism, including racial taunts, from neighborhood bullies.[4] And after Gim's father died, the responsibility for his mother and six siblings fell squarely on his shoulders.[5] He was fourteen years old and about to enter his sophomore year of high school.

Gim also assumed responsibility for his father's share in the Nan King Lo restaurant in Beloit. Before his father died, Gim had worked in the kitchen at the restaurant, and he tried to continue that, in addition to taking on the responsibilities of ownership. Thus he worked well into the night, and his job as part owner required him to take home the cash after the restaurant closed each day. He would then rise early the next morning and ride his bicycle to the bank to deposit the previous night's earnings. Gim gave that up when he started back at school. It was simply too difficult for the full-time high school student to work those kinds of hours. Consequently, Yee Shee sold her husband's share in the restaurant. Gim continued to work and, with an eye to his future, he secured summertime employment at the wood working machine manufacturer, Yates American. When he graduated from high school in 1942, Gim became an apprentice machinist at Yates.[6]

Whatever feelings Gim must have had for his own loss and his mother's suffering, his grief had little effect on the quality of his schoolwork or extracurricular involvement in high school. He excelled in math, shop, and mechanical drawing, in addition to civics, history, and chemistry. His grades in Latin, biology, and English were only slightly lower. His teachers nominated him to the National Honor Society, and his peers elected him treasurer of his class.[7] Applying to college, his high school counselor praised Gim as "a very exceptional young man well-liked by all."[8] He must have been a good friend, too, for he later recounted that his best friend recruited him to help with the high school yearbook. Though neither had any idea what the job entailed when they signed on to the project, they worked hard on it and earned an "A" rating when the book was entered in a contest at the University of Minnesota.[9] Gim's high school record set a high standard to which his siblings aspired.

The U.S. Army drafted Gim in World War II, and he served as a staff sergeant for two years.[10] He started basic training in November 1944 and was deployed in Leyte, in the Philippines, for eighteen months, serving as a mechanic and motor pool driver.[11] Although Gim did not talk openly about his experiences in the service, he would have been a reinforcement in the campaign to recapture the American colony from the Japanese. He would also have been in the Philippines for the dropping of the atom bombs on Hiroshima and Nagasaki in August 1945 and would have celebrated VJ Day on August 15 and Japan's surrender on September 2, 1945.

Gim set his intention to go to college while he was in the service. He later said that when he was in the army and in the shop at Yates American,

Gim and George Wong, 1940s. (David Palmer)

he "noticed that the man with the college degree was usually the one who held the best and most important position." That man, Gim noted, "could usually choose what he wanted, while others merely had to take what was given them."[12] After his discharge, he followed his younger brother, George, to Beloit College, where he studied for a year—living at home to save on room and board—before transferring to the University of Wisconsin–Madison using GI Bill funds.[13] Gim graduated as a mechanical engineer in 1951, the same year as his cousin Terry Lee.[14] They would be the first of the large Wong clan to earn university degrees.

As the eldest son, it fell to Gim to advise and assist his mother in leading the family. Now that his father had passed, Gim assumed his place as co-owner of the apartments in Hong Kong.[15] In 1948 twenty-four-year-old Gim accompanied his mother to Hong Kong to help her sell two properties to raise money for the family back in Beloit. The Hong Kong economy was recovering from wartime occupation by the Japanese, and it benefitted from the Allied presence in China. They sold their share in the properties on Egg Street and on Hennessy Road but retained a share in a final property on Hennessy. Unable to repatriate the kind of money they earned in the transaction, Yee Shee chose a traditional Chinese method of wealth retention; she returned to Beloit with jade, gems, and silk. She distributed these as gifts to her children and her sons' future brides.

Gim's close relationship to his mother continued throughout his adult life. When they traveled to Boston for Frank's graduation, for example, Gim took Yee Shee to Boston's Chinatown to look for her oldest brother, whom she had not seen since she left China in 1923. After an arduous search, they found him in a rooming house, alive but unwell. He died soon after.[16]

One important divide between the two "generations" of siblings was their choice of marriage partner, a choice that was fraught with cultural expectations and judgments. Yee Shee Wong made it clear to her children that she wanted them to marry Chinese or Chinese Americans. Growing up American, however, the Wong children found the idea of marriage brokers and matchmaking antiquated. They knew very few young Chinese or Asian people, and the ones they did meet often had very different cultural experiences and expectations. There was much kidding among the siblings in 1948 that one

Gim Wong and
Mother Wong in
Hong Kong, 1948.
(David Palmer)

of Yee Shee's goals in Hong Kong was to find a matchmaker for Gim. But
he was too Americanized at that point and refused to go along with Yee
Shee's plan.

Even though Americans tell themselves that marriage is about romantic
love and individual choice, the size and makeup of the pool of suitable marriage partners is determined by law and by cultural norms. In 1954 interracial
marriage was illegal in seventeen of the forty-eight states.[17] Wisconsin was
one of only nine states that had never implemented anti-miscegenation laws,
laws that made it illegal to marry someone of a different race, but interracial

dating and marriage were nevertheless frowned upon. Gim Wong experienced the humiliation of having the father of a girl he dated at Beloit College—"a lawyer from Chicago, a man with a red hot temper"—bang on the door of his mother's house to threaten him if he continued to date his daughter.[18] But one effect of decades of Asian exclusion from immigration was the scarcity of Chinese and Chinese American women throughout the country, and especially in the Midwest.[19]

Gim was the first of the Wong siblings to marry, and he married a Wisconsin woman of German descent. Marion Marie Erdman had grown up on a farm in Jefferson, Wisconsin, and attended Whitewater State College (later University of Wisconsin–Whitewater) to become a teacher. Afterward she moved to Beloit and got a job at Merrill School. Gim was with friends at Buffa's Supper Club, a restaurant in the Illinois town of South Beloit, when he met Marion and her friends there in 1953. The story goes that when Gim asked if he could drop Marion off afterward, she thought he was very forward, but she did allow it.[20] They were married at St. Paul's Lutheran Church in Fort Atkinson, Wisconsin, in June 1954, in a wedding that reflected Marion's cultural background and expectations. The tall, stylish Marion wore a white rose patterned Chantilly lace over a basque bodiced dress with a bouffant, waltz-length skirt. In the bridal party were Gim's brother George as best man and Marion's sister Ruth as maid of honor. Gim's sister, Helen Wong, and Marion's sister, Marjorie Erdman, were also bridesmaids; and Gim's best friends from high school, Bob Cox and Ralph "Bill" Babcock, were groomsmen.[21] Gim and Marion went on to raise four children—Ann, Wendy, Michael, and John—born between 1956 and 1966.

The family suffered a terrible tragedy in 1969 that offers insight into Gim's character. The family was moving into their nearly completed home on Garfield Street in Beloit. Gim's two little boys were playing with a balloon in the living room of the house. A rope divided the room, separating off the area by the fireplace hearth, which was still under construction. When six-year-old Michael chased a balloon to the other side of the rope, a stone on the fireplace hearth dislodged, falling on the child and killing him. It was immediately apparent that the contractor was at fault since Gim had notified him about the loose masonry a week before the family moved in. Gim knew the

Gim, Ann, Wendy, Marion, John, and Michael Wong, 1968. (David Palmer)

contractor well and knew how bad the man felt about his error. The family was devastated by Michael's death. When asked later why he didn't sue the man, Gim said, "Why should I ruin somebody else's life by suing him? Mine is already ruined."[22] His reluctance to retaliate allows a fuller understanding of Gim's maturity and equanimity toward others.

Gim balanced his need to raise his family close by his mother with leadership positions at work and in the Beloit community. After he graduated from the University of Wisconsin, he worked as an industrial engineer at Yates American and as a manager of plant engineering at Warner Electric Brake & Clutch Co. In 1967 Gim was named plant engineering manager at Fairbanks, Morse and Company, the engine maker. He was employed as a foundry engineer at Beloit Corporation at the time of his death, in 1991. Gim was active in professional societies, the American Foundrymen's Society and the American Institution of Plant Engineers, and his quiet authority at work and involvement in the community led him to seek public office. He was elected to the local school board in 1970, where he served for nine years, including four as vice president and two as president. Other positions speak to his dedication to the community: eight years on the City of Beloit Planning Commission and membership on the PTAs of his children's schools. The city named him Beloit Booster of the Year in 1971.[23]

Gim played a role in the larger movement to end associational racial discrimination following the war. An excellent bowler, Gim bowled with the UAW-CIO, local 77 team that entered the state bowling tournament in 1947. After they registered for the tournament, however, organizers informed the team that they were disqualified because the American Bowling Congress allowed "white males only" to bowl. UAW-CIO held a meeting in Chicago to discuss the rules and founded the group National Committee for Fair Play in Bowling (CFPB), chaired by then-Mayor of Minneapolis, Hubert Humphrey. Gim's wartime service made his exclusion especially appalling to World War II veterans, and the CFPB filed anti-discrimination suits in Illinois, New York, and Wisconsin. In 1950 Judge A. Sbarbaro of the Illinois Supreme Court ruled against the American Bowling Congress and fined it $2,500.[24] Thus one of Gim Wong's legacies is that he desegregated the sport of bowling in the United States.

Gim's children learned from their dad not so much by direct instruction as by following his example. They remember him as a man of integrity who valued humility, thrift, and community service.[25] He was humble, his son said, "although he enjoyed the limelight, he didn't seek it out." Gim was also notoriously cheap. With wry Wong humor very much on display, John Wong said the rickety ladder his dad had him use to clean out the eaves of Grandmother Wong's house in the early 1970s "had probably come with them on the boat" from China fifty years earlier. One value that John learned from Gim was giving back to the community, which he did in his service on the Beloit School Board, where he served as interim president and member for several years. Gim would certainly be proud of John and his wife, Becky, for mentoring and fostering high school kids from the local schools. For his part, John says he sees a reflection of his father's experiences in the local community:

> Even as we speak, the way my grandmother raised her kids is the same as how immigrant kids are raised today in Beloit. Immigrants who are poor, hardworking,

with integrity and broken English. They hide in the shadows. They know education is the one thing nobody can take away from you.

Serving Family and Community: Fung

As the eldest daughter, Fung Wong felt the burden of dual expectations of her Chinese mother and American society. Writing about second-generation Chinese Americans, scholar Sucheng Chan has noted that Chinese American daughters' restrictive ethnic cultures played a more dominant role in their identity formation than race, which was more salient for men.[26] Fung definitely faced gendered expectations. Even before her father's death, Fung had certain obligations in the family from which her brothers were exempt, especially babysitting, but also helping her mother with domestic chores like scrubbing the floor, mending, and cooking. Yet Fung's experiences show that she claimed a similar amount of self-determination over her adult life as her brothers did, pursuing a professional education, becoming a successful nurse, and marrying whom she chose.[27]

Her position as one of the two oldest children set an obligation to be a role model for the younger siblings too. High achievement in school offered a bridge between cultural expectations of her parents and the society she grew up in. Like Gim, Fung was elected to leadership positions in high school and performed as "an outstanding student."[28] As a worker in local variety stores during high school, moreover, her leadership skills were noticed and remunerated. It is worth noting that the prewar job experiences Fung had as the first Chinese American woman seeking work in her small city in the Midwest were different than experiences of her Chinese American peers in West Coast cities, who were steered to domestic service or working in Chinese-owned businesses.[29] In the area of suitability for employment, there was less discrimination against Fung as a young Chinese American woman in Beloit than there was for young African American women.[30]

Fung had professional aspirations, too. She desperately wanted to become a nurse and knew she had what it took to do so, but with her father gone and barely enough money to feed and clothe her siblings, there was no way the family could afford to send her to nursing school. A wartime opportunity came at exactly the right time.

World War II brought an acute need for qualified American nurses. Starting in September 1943, the Madison General Hospital School of Nursing, which had closed for several years during the Depression, operated a three-year diploma program to train members of the U.S. Cadet Nurse Corps. Located in the Wisconsin state capital, just an hour away from her home, this program gave Fung the opportunity to pursue a dream—"the opportunity to attend nursing school with all expenses paid."[31] She had wanted to become a nurse ever since an experience she'd had when she was ten years old. Her brother Gim had split his lip in football practice and needed a few stiches, and Fung accompanied him to the hospital. When the family doctor invited her into the room with Gim, Fung was struck by the cleanliness of the room and instruments.

Joining the Cadet Nurse program allowed Fung to have a college experience away from the small city where she had so many responsibilities. The cadets were housed in a remodeled four-story house in Madison, complete with a house mother and very strict rules, including a 10:00 p.m. curfew and lights out at 11:00. They studied hard in the program, but they also enjoyed each other's company, played bridge, and went canoeing in Lake Wingra between shifts in the hospital. A six-month rotation in pediatrics at Cook County Hospital in Chicago in 1947 provided both clinical experience—she saw the bloated body of a corpse pulled out of the Chicago River—and social experience. In addition to working in a crime-ridden depressed economic community, she also had her "first exposure to the gay community" in Chicago when she was invited to a meeting hosted by lesbians who were fellow students in the nursing program. These kinds of encounters with diverse peoples and cultures were a hallmark of many young people's experience of service and travel in wartime America.[32]

Fung experienced a more diverse set of colleagues and contacts and made a lifelong friend of Alice Noguchi. On the first day of the nursing program, the nursing director summoned Fung to her office. Facing the stern Nurse Ida Collings—the "stiffly starched uniformed, prim, Johns Hopkins–trained director of nurses"—Fung wondered what rules she might have broken already. She was surprised when Nurse Collings asked if she would be amenable to being in training with a nurse who had come directly from a Japanese "relocation camp" in Arizona. One of the only ways out of the detention camps for these American citizens of Japanese descent was to join the military or, for young women, to join a program like the Cadet Nurse Corps. Knowing that China and Japan were at war, Nurse Collings said she hoped Fung could work alongside a woman of Japanese ancestry. From her perspective, Fung felt that making a request like that showed Nurse Collings's obtuseness about race. As an eighteen-year-old, U.S.–born American raised in Wisconsin, what experience would Fung have had that would have made her feel animosity toward another eighteen-year-old American?[33] On the other hand, once she indicated that it would not be a problem, the program placed the young woman on the same floor of the dormitory in a room adjacent to

Cadet Nurse program advertisement, U.S. Public Health Service, 1944. (University of North Texas)

Fung's. Perhaps they were seen as sharing a single racial category, and the hope was that the two women would offer each other solidarity. And in fact, that is what happened. Alice Noguchi became one of Fung's "true friends."[34] Decisions like these are what led to the forging of a distinct Asian American identity.

Not long after she became a registered nurse, Fung helped open the first emergency room in Beloit, in 1948. She had been working as a surgical nurse at Beloit Hospital with Dr. Kasten when she dropped a syringe during a surgical procedure. When a supervisor, Nurse Florence, berated her in front of the doctor and a groggy patient, which was a breach of medical conduct, Fung took offense and resigned immediately. There were plenty of opportunities in the wartime economy, and she applied to be a nurse at the huge Fairbanks-Morse industrial complex. That same day, the director of nurses at Beloit Hospital, Mary Evans, called Fung to say she had been watching her

Fung Wong, nursing school grad, 1947. (Fung Scholz)

since she started and wanted her to help open the new emergency room. Fung worked at Beloit Hospital full-time for two years. In 1950 she moved with her friend Alice to Milwaukee to try to finish her bachelor's degree at Marquette University.[35] She gave up that plan a short time later to return to Beloit and marry. Subsequently, she worked part-time as a surgical and industrial nurse at several institutions in Beloit.

Fung's marriage to a non-Chinese man caused a falling-out between her and her mother. Although her mother had been fairly tolerant of her spending time in groups with Gim's friends, and dating his friend Bill Babcock in high school, Yee Shee let Fung know in no uncertain terms that she expected her to marry a man of Chinese descent. Fung had a less-public (than Gim) but very upsetting experience when Bill, with whom she corresponded during his wartime military service, came to Madison during his leave from paratrooper service in Alaska to tell her he had to break it off because his parents did not approve of her because she was Chinese. His announcement came as a terrible shock to Fung, who loved Bill and had expected the relationship would lead to marriage.

Fung made real efforts to find a suitable mate, according to her mother's standards, but she found too vast the cultural gap between her suitors' expectations and her own. Fung joined the Chinese Club at the University of Wisconsin–Madison, where she met male Chinese students from Hong Kong. They did not appreciate her Americanized ways.[36] They seemed to want only to talk and never to listen, especially if she were trying to express a strong or deeply felt opinion. She did not find they offered much as partners either. They did not hold jobs, and their prospects for working and providing a home and family after graduation seemed meager.[37] When she was in nurse's training in Chicago, Fung dated a man named Joe Leong from Guangdong province. Her mother loved Joe, but Fung's brothers dismissively called him "Joe Blow" for his long-windedness, and Fung ultimately decided he couldn't settle down enough to start a family.[38] In the end, Fung felt more comfortable with the Western approach to dating. She appreciated the everyday kindness, respect, and mutual support she felt in relationships with men who had not been raised in China. Back in Beloit, Fung dated a neighbor from the next block, Elwood "Al" Scholz, an American of German ancestry.

Al was an engineer at Fairbanks, Morse and Company for more than thirty years, a multilingual World War I veteran who acted as a warden during the World War II blackouts in Beloit.[39] Fung decided to marry him in spite of her mother's opposition to the relationship, and the two eloped to Gary, Indiana, on November 5, 1951. This caused a major rift between Fung and her mother.

Yee Shee's opposition was mainly about Al's ethnicity, though the relationship likely reminded her how powerless she would be over certain aspects of her children's lives. Yee Shee harbored hopes that all of her children would marry Chinese mates. Since she knew the urban areas had eligible young Chinese men, Yee Shee thought her daughters would find spouses in the United States and her sons would return to Hong Kong or China to find suitable spouses.[40] Marriage was one of the most important events of a young person's life, so significant for Chinese men that they took on a permanent name

Mother Wong and her oldest grandson, Alan Scholz, 1952. (David Palmer)

afterward. Marriage was so important for young Chinese women that they cut nearly all ties to their families of origin and joined their husband's family. Thus Fung's marriage came as a great shock to Yee Shee, and she was unable to even speak to Fung for several months. That Fung and Al remained nearby and started a family right away provided the reason to patch things up. They reconciled when Fung and Al's first child, Alan Guy Scholz, was born in 1952.

The reality was that Fung's marriage to a neighbor improved Yee Shee's life in unexpected ways. Living on the next block facilitated the close relationship between Fung's children Alan, Mary, and Cherie and their grandmother. Fung's daughter Mary, who is Yee Shee's oldest granddaughter, has many happy memories of time spent with Yee Shee.[41] Fung describes her mother "racing over" when she saw that the family car was in the driveway. Furthermore, not only did Yee Shee not "lose" her daughter to marriage, as she would have in China, but Fung continued to help her mother out as she

Fung and Al (standing at right) with Alan, Mary, and Cherie Scholz with their extended family in Beloit, 1975. (Bill Wong)

aged, an extension of the expectation she had in her youth. Fung and her children all describe this relationship as extremely rewarding.[42]

Fung's children recognize especially her strength of character. From a very young age she expressed the values she had internalized at home in Beloit: love and support of family, hard work, and giving back to the community. Like her elder brother Gim and younger brother George, Fung spent her teen years supporting her mother and younger siblings. In adulthood she stayed close to her mother in spite of her mother's disappointment that she hadn't married a Chinese man. She is proud of her children's closeness and of her extended family.[43] Fung's dedication to hard work allowed her to excel in her chosen profession, working at Beloit Hospital, opening its first emergency room, and working in private duty and industrial nursing. She employed these skills to nurse her husband at home for years in the latter part of his life. She volunteered at the blood bank and city health department while raising her children. And in her retirement, Fung has continued to participate enthusiastically in her community.

George: Service to Family and Work

Having exceeded low expectations as a sickly boy, George (Wong Gim Ham) came into his own in high school. This handsome, popular boy dreamed of having a successful career that would help his mother out. After the ROTC in high school and college, George became an electrical engineer with a broad choice of jobs in the postwar industrial economy.

His siblings remember that their mother babied George, who was "a very thin child without much energy," because of his asthma. Their mother made "smelly" herbal remedies for George to inhale and seemed to always offer him the choicest parts of the single chicken that the family of eight shared.[44] His childhood was not all about sitting around being waited on, however; in the time he spent indoors, George played with wooden building blocks and an erector set, creating machines powered by a motor. Only nine and a half years old when his father died, George had had to grow up quickly.[45]

Like his siblings, George's primary goal was to help his mother make ends meet. He took on a paper route for the *Milwaukee Journal* at age twelve and worked through high school as a soda jerk (for twenty-five cents per hour) at

Liberty Pharmacy, the neighborhood drug store. On Sundays George brought home butter pecan ice cream for the family to eat after their fried chicken and baked potato dinner.[46] He outgrew his infirmities in high school, and took on leadership roles that included student council, the ROTC, yearbook, the Red Cross, and president of Hi-Y as a senior.[47] The latter role helped him earn a Hi-Y scholarship to college. George felt well-supported by his community. The day he graduated from Beloit Memorial High School, principal James H. McNeel called George into his office to give him a set of professional drawing instruments because he knew George planned to go into engineering.[48] George said he used the instruments all through his university career.

Like Gim and Fung, George parlayed military service, during the Korean War, into access to higher education. His aptitude for math, drawing, and mechanics allowed George to dream of a career in engineering. For one year between high school and college, he worked on locomotives at Fairbanks, Morse and Company and saved his money for college. Living at home, George attended Beloit College for one year before transferring to the University of Wisconsin–Madison to major in electrical engineering.[49] He remembered taking a "great," year-long class in Introductory Physics with Ron Palmer, years before his sister Mary met Ron's son David.[50] In the Cold War era of science and technology rivalry with the Soviet Union and China, engineering was a critical skill for the nation, with estimates in 1948 that the United States needed to train 150,000 young men at the bachelor's level.[51] The federal government poured money into training in the sciences and engineering. When North Korean troops crossed the 38th parallel on June 25, 1950, the army called up reservists and National Guard troops, resumed the draft, and shifted additional resources into university training programs like the ROTC.[52] George joined the ROTC for two years at the University of Wisconsin–Madison beginning in 1950, which protected him from the draft while he was a university student—in exchange for an agreement to serve—and enabled him to serve as an officer when he joined the army immediately following his graduation.[53] At a time when tuition cost $50 per semester at UW–Madison, George remembers earning $50 or $60 a month in the ROTC. He was proud to lead the honor guard and band onto the field at home football games at the University of Wisconsin.[54]

In 1952 George was one of 143 University of Wisconsin–Madison graduates who "stepped out of their caps and gowns right into uniforms," graduating in February and entering service in April.[55] After training at Fort
Belvoir in Virginia and Fort Leonard Wood in Missouri, the army sent Second Lieutenant George Wong to Busan, Korea, where he served as an oper-
ations officer in an engineering utility detachment for fourteen months in
the Army Corps of Engineers.[56] During the war the unit installed security
perimeter lighting in all of the U.S. Army bases in Korea. After the armi-
stice was signed between the United States, North Korea, and China in July
1953, the unit worked with the civilian Korean Electric and Power Company
to maintain power lines and ration power. George supervised three civilian Korean engineers and a crew of fifty Koreans in that time, ending his
service in February 1954 as First Lieutenant. George credited the service
for allowing him to develop skills in supervising and in project travel and
management.[57]

Second Lieutenant George
Wong, 1952. (Bill Wong)

George met Joyce Ann Morrow in college at the University of Wisconsin–Madison. They met at a Chadbourne Dormitory open house, introduced by George's younger sister Helen, and they dated for only one semester before George went to Korea. The two wrote to each other nearly every day when George was in the service, exploring such topics as faith—he was an unenthusiastic Presbyterian and she was a passionate Catholic—and the possibility of a future together.[58] In a letter from San Francisco written as he was shipping out to Korea, George implored Joyce to have the courage to be honest with him about their relationship and not to mislead him during his deployment.[59] The two married on July 17, 1954, in the chapel at Durward's Glen, site of a Catholic seminary near Joyce's hometown of Merrimac, Wisconsin. Younger sister Mary Wong was a bridesmaid alongside Joyce's friend Patsy Tschanz, while brother Gim Wong served as a groomsman with Joyce's brother, Gene Morrow. Following an afternoon reception on the seminary grounds, George and Joyce drove Gim's 1952 Chevrolet to Niagara Falls for a weeklong honeymoon.[60]

George Wong and Joyce Morrow correspondence, 1950s. (Becca Fortsch)

George's career as an engineering manager in Beloit Iron Works (later Beloit Corporation) dovetailed with the company's peak production. He had begun his career by designing electric motors and generators at Fairbanks, but in 1957 Beloit Iron Works hired him as an electrical engineer. Over the next thirty-six years, he took assignments at various Beloit Corporation subsidiaries as he rose through their management structure.[61] Throughout his career, George traveled to install Beloit Corporation's paper machines. One trip in 1975 took him 22,000 miles around the world, from Beloit west to Bangkok, Thailand, where he worked at Beloit Corp's paper mills, and back to the U.S. via Delhi, India, and Frankfurt, Germany.[62] A *Beloit Daily News* article in 1969 identified him as "a recognized authority in the areas of supercalender design and operation," refining processes in papermaking. By the end of his career, George had amassed three patents for paper machine technology.[63]

Staying in the Midwest for much of his career, George joined Gim and Fung as primary caregivers for their mother, choices that allowed the younger four siblings to accept positions outside of the region.[64] As Mary later wrote to George, "We younger siblings never had the responsibilities that you three older ones assumed after our father's death and that continued until [Mother's] death in 1978. She was able to live in her own home as she wished to the end."[65] In 1958 Yee Shee even purchased a home across the street from her house where George and Joyce lived for two years.[66] This proximity allowed close relationships to develop between Yee Shee and George and Joyce's children, William, born 1955; Robert, 1957; Richard, 1958; David, 1960; Catherine, 1961; and Lisa, 1967, who lived nearby.[67] Early in their lives, Yee Shee babysat several of the older grandchildren, but even the younger ones described relationships developed through daily, weekly, or monthly visits.[68]

George's legacy is undoubtedly as a role model. As a young man he modeled family loyalty, responsibility, and self-discipline to his younger siblings.[69] As a father, he focused on these but placed family at the center. "[My parents] helped me understand the love of family," wrote his son Bill, the eldest of six children. "It is the one thing I hope I have passed on to my kids and grandkids with my wife, Ann. Part of this included taking the family on trips where we visited grandparents and met cousins, aunts, and uncles. Reunions

June 24, 1969

George Wong

Wong Gets Promotion in Beloit Group

George Wong has been named general manager of the Wheeler Division of the Beloit Corp., it was announced today by M. W. Johnson, division vice president. The operation is located in Kalamazoo, Mich.

Wong has been associated with the Beloit Group 15 years. He served as staff engineer in Beloit prior to his transfer to the Paper Finishing Machinery Division in Downingtown, Pa., in 1960. He has served as chief engineer at Downingtown since 1965.

A recognized authority in the areas of supercalender design and operation, Wong is a member of TAPPIs Calendering and Finishing Committee. He is scheduled to present a paper on the subject of supercalender drives at the TAPPI engineering conference in September 1969.

Beloit Daily News clipping, 1969. (George Ham Wong application folder, Beloit College Archives)

George, Richard, Bill, Joyce with Lisa, Cathy, and David, 1970. (Lisa Fortsch)

were a way to celebrate the family and were events we still remember 'til this day."[70] George imparted a passion for education, scouts, sports, electronics, tinkering, and finance.[71] He taught his children to work hard and to keep their expectations high.[72] He inspired his son Bill to become an electrical engineer, teaching him basic electrical work, soldering, and schematics as a child.[73] Coupled with high expectations was his ability to really listen and to help them overcome an obstacle or achieve a goal.[74] Daughter Cathy Wong Ring is grateful for his advice, useful in her personal life and in the workplace, to worry only about things she could control, in order to remain positive and focused.[75] All of his children remember him as a stern parent, though son David suggested his behavior warranted it.[76] One expression daughter Lisa recalls George saying is, "There are no mulligans, even in life," emphasizing his expectation that his children would do their best to get things right the first time.[77]

Coming of age during World War II and the Korean War, the older Wong siblings' careers were closely tied to national service. This was by choice, but it was also practical because funding and programs related to national service existed to support their college aspirations. Gim and George both served active duty overseas; Fung was trained for that service and gave in other ways. Having grown up in a small city whose industries and services embraced their skills and talents—unlike what Chinese Americans faced in larger cities in the same era—they also felt called to give back to that community in their adulthood. Their talents were rewarded in the booming wartime economy of Beloit and, for George, other cities where Beloit Corporation had factories. Gim was elected to public office; Gim and George served on professional boards; and Fung served for decades in community organizations. Their sense of community service came from a lifetime of serving their family: as the older children, Gim, Fung, and George rose to the expectation that they would model Chinese values for their siblings, which included stepping into a parental role with their younger siblings when their father died.

CHAPTER FIVE

Part of a National Community

Helen, Harry, Frank, and Mary Wong

The younger Wong siblings, although they stayed close to their mother and prioritized relations with the extended family, became professionals and raised families outside of the Midwest. Each one used the same pathway to success in childhood and young adulthood that the older siblings had paved: excellence in academics, internalized traditional Chinese values, earning money to help out the family, and community involvement. These siblings came of age in the 1950s, when industrial production had peaked and regional and national economies had changed. Part of a new generation of American college graduates, they sought national and international opportunities. They experienced predominately European-American cultural expectations but also interacted more and formed their identities among Chinese, Asian Americans, and international individuals and groups outside of the Midwest.

In many ways, Beloit, Wisconsin, in the 1950s provided a welcoming community for the high-achieving Wong children. Everyone in the city of 30,000 knew them, it seemed. People had known and loved their father and/or his restaurant, or they knew their older brothers Gim or George from work, or sister Fung from the hospital. The family reputation was built on honesty, humility, diligence, and dependability.[1] Although all of the children had experienced racism in childhood, Harry and Mary reported they saw less of it in high school because of the strong family reputation.[2] Mary's story, in particular, offers a contrast to the social exclusion and discrimination Chinese

American teens faced in West Coast cities in the 1950s, and speaks to the strength of the Beloit community. It is evident from their high school records that their peers thought the Wongs exceptional.[3] In a public high school with more than 320 students in each graduating class, the youngest four siblings, beginning with Helen Wong in 1949, were voted "most likely to succeed." The school was predominately white at the time, of mixed middle- and working-class backgrounds, with 5 percent African American and just one or two Asian American graduates in each class. To say the younger Wongs were active in high school is an understatement—three of the four younger siblings were voted "busiest senior."[4] They were friendly, well-rounded, hardworking, popular kids. As they finished high school in Beloit, they sought opportunities in the changing national economy, forming identities, finding partners, and establishing families outside of the Midwest.

Family, Intersectional Identity, and Cooking: Helen

Helen (Wong Fung Sem) was freer from family expectations than her older sister Fung had been, but she faced other challenges. Creative, outgoing, brilliant, and beautiful, Helen was a whirlwind of motion in adulthood. Her ambition to grow beyond the limitations of midwestern expectations of a Chinese American woman was realized. Letters to the Round Robin (a circulating family newsletter) and private letters home detail a busy travel schedule, cooking classes, and leadership in the International Women's Society in Pullman, Washington, where she lived with her family from 1967 to 1982.[5]

Born in 1931, Helen was a high achiever at Beloit High School. Like her older siblings, her classmates elected her to student government, and her teachers selected her for the National Honor Society. In 1948, out of the 272 girls in the American Legion Auxiliary Girls State program, she was one of two senators elected to represent Wisconsin at the ALA Girls Nation in Washington, DC, where she had the opportunity to meet President Truman.[6] Helen worked at a local dime store, Kresge's, throughout high school. She attended the University of Wisconsin–Madison where she became an occupational therapist and was later recruited to teach in the Occupational Therapy Program there.[7]

Like her older and younger siblings, Helen felt the sting of anti-Chinese racism in love. The man she had dated through high school, Terry Bassett, informed her after she began college that his parents opposed their relationship. His father specifically objected to how difficult he imagined life as a mixed-race person would be for the future generation.[8] The rejection was, in a way, a rejection of the whole Wong family because the Wongs and Bassetts had been close.[9] Although Helen later professed that she'd had doubts about his fitness as her partner because he was "so lax and without initiative," she also confessed to her sister that she "really had planned to marry him."[10] Helen had other painful experiences of loss of relationships in early adulthood, including with a man named Bryan whom she met in Portland, Oregon, and followed to Washington, DC, where the relationship ended.[11] Helen suffered an episode of severe depression. Her brothers responded, led by Gim. He sent Frank from Boston to visit Helen in Washington, DC, and insisted she return home, where Harry helped find medical care for her. After

Frank, Mary, and Helen
Wong, 1944. (David Palmer)

a brief hospitalization, Helen was at home recovering when Jim Way came calling.

James Leong Way was a match for Helen's indomitable spirit. Jim's family had also emigrated from Guangdong—but to Oakland, California—and his family was similarly fun loving if, as Helen's brother Frank said, "noisier about it." Frank lovingly described Jim as "versatile, good humored, aggressive, opportunistic, athletic, and materialistic."[12] When they met, Jim was in a post-doctoral pharmacology position at the University of Wisconsin Medical School, having graduated from George Washington University in Washington, DC. Jim's Chinese friends told him about a woman from their community of friends who had recently returned to Wisconsin. True to his character, Jim drove the hour from Madison to Beloit without an introduction and cold-called at Yee Shee's door. He did not come empty-handed: he brought Chinese language newspapers and food, likely the reason Yee Shee invited him in.[13] The family story goes that when Fung came downstairs with baby

Helen Wong, University of Wisconsin–Madison, 1953. (David Palmer)

Alan in her arms, Jim thought, "too late." Then Helen, uninterested in talking to a man who showed up at the door out of the blue, had to be cajoled down from upstairs. After many months of courting—using the excuse of driving younger sister Mary, then a student at the University of Wisconsin, back and forth from Madison to Beloit, and stopping by the house with gifts to talk to Yee Shee—Jim slowly won Helen's heart.

Helen and Jim's wedding on June 23, 1957, celebrated their Chinese American backgrounds. Paper umbrellas and lanterns adorned the room for the reception, held in the basement of the West Side Presbyterian Church in Beloit at 11th Street and Liberty. Helen had designed a cake with an Asian motif of red and gold colors: red for good luck and gold for prosperity. Punch and cookies were also served. An artifact of this celebration, a meticulous listing of items and expenses for the costs of the wedding, including dresses for the bride and attendants, tux rentals, the church, and reception, shows that the total cost of the wedding was less than $400.[14] Careful budgeting had helped this family survive the impoverished circumstances of their Depression-era childhood, and it would be decades before members of this generation felt they could afford not to count every penny of expenses.[15]

Helen experienced an intense "intersectional" struggle as a woman and as a person of color in America. Intersectionality examines the ways multiple aspects of an individual's identity affect their development and life.[16] The lived experiences of an Asian American woman will be different than those of an Asian American man or a white American woman. Jennifer Ho argues that the examination of intersectionality is especially meaningful in Asian American studies, particularly "the ways these various identities are not simply additive but comprise overlapping and sometimes contradictory statuses of oppression and privilege."[17] Gender and race each affected Helen in overlapping and interdependent ways. As a woman who came of age in the 1950s, she had to subsume her ambitions and love of travel under her husband's. They did take many trips together, but Jim traveled constantly for work. Meanwhile, racially she had felt "different" than her white peers for all her teenage and young adult life in Beloit and Madison, which affected her identity. She was thrilled to meet an "Oriental crowd" in Portland and Hawaii. She expressed these feelings to younger sister Mary:

When I was on the coast and in Portland and in Hawaii, I was in with a completely Oriental crowd. There is an inexplicable feeling of really belonging—not
that I ever felt out of place with Caucasians. But there's something that came over
me that makes me appreciate more the Chinese culture and people and to be a part
of them. I felt so wanted and so much at home in the many places I visited and
homes I was invited to. Their hospitality overwhelmed me and, as I say, it's a hard
feeling to convey. You have never seen Chinatown SF [San Francisco] or ever experienced being with Chinese Americans. It's different—anyways to me. At the university I met and dated Chinese, but they were all from China and I didn't get along
with them.[18]

As part of Helen's rotation to become an occupational therapist, she traveled and spent time in Seattle, Portland, San Francisco, and Hawaii. Each
place Helen went, she was appreciated for her professional and social skills;
in each city she found friends and suitors among the Asian and mixed-race
populations.

Helen talked the most about her experiences in Hawaii. When she was
leaving the site in Hawaii, her patients didn't want to see her go. They threw
a party and gifted her with a "big, beautiful fifties-style rotisserie." Her children remember Helen cooking chickens on it but especially how the rotisserie itself reminded their mother "that people loved her . . . even though she
was only there for a little while." She really felt she belonged in Hawaii, with
its mixed-race population. She named her oldest daughter Lani for her love
of that time.[19] Finding a place where she felt comfortable among other Asian
Americans, where she felt "so much at home," must have convinced her that
marrying a Chinese American man, especially one who would pursue her to
the extent Jim Way did, would bring that level of comfort and acceptance.

After they married, Helen and Jim lived in Madison together before they
moved to the Milwaukee area for Jim's job at Marquette University Medical
School (which later became the Medical College of Wisconsin). Helen loved
modern design and the couple purchased a home with a flat roof and open
floor plan that had been designed by a renowned regional architect.[20] The
family remembers Yee Shee referred to the spacious home as the "big club-
house" because it had a wall of windows and looked out over a woods and

pasture. In Madison, their daughter Lani had been born in 1958, their son Jon in 1960, and Lori in 1964, before they moved to Brookfield, Wisconsin. A little more than an hour from Beloit, the Ways were close to their grand-mother and cousins until 1967, when Washington State University at Pullman, in eastern Washington, recruited Jim for a job.

The Ways loved a good joke. When they lived in Brookfield, they roasted a pig for the Wong clan one Christmas. Since they knew how much Helen's younger sister, Mary, enjoyed roasted pig, Helen told Mary about it when-ever the family roasted a pig after that. One day upon returning home after a full day of teaching, Mary opened an airmailed, special delivery package from them. Inside was the head of their roasted pig, with an apple in its mouth and cherries in its eyes. Not to be outdone, Mary and her husband, David, scraped every bit of meat and skin from the pig and mailed it back to them.[21]

Helen's activities in Pullman reflect her identity as a Chinese American and her embrace of the limited roles available to university wives of the era.

Lori, Lani, Helen, Jim, and Jon Way, 1974. (David Palmer)

She started an international women's club at Pullman, eventually becoming its president. Even while she chafed at feeling isolated there, Helen had dozens of friends in Pullman. She earned extra money and media attention by offering popular Chinese cooking classes. In 1977 she published a cookbook with a title that pokes fun at her maiden and married names: *Chinese Cooking the Wong Way*. It was a family project; Helen invited her children to help design the chapter headings and draw pictures that cleverly hid the artists' initials. She also included recipes from her mother, sister, and sisters-in-law. She dedicated the book to her three teenagers: "May [this cookbook] enhance their appreciation of their cultural heritage as exemplified by its

Chinese Cooking the Wong Way, 1977. (David Palmer)

cuisine." As her mother taught her to do, Helen expressed eternal love and nurturing for her children and their Chinese heritage through cooking.

Helen was the first family historian: as an adult she reached out to extended family and began to piece together the complicated history of their parents' lives. She expressed surprise that one person she spoke to, a man she knew to be a relative, denied the family connection and claimed to be "good friends" of the family. This discovery led her to ask questions about the history of Chinese exclusion and paper sons. She sought additional stories from extended and elder family members.[22]

Weekends at the coast provided a respite from the busy life in Pullman, especially when Yee Shee, who loved the water and fishing, visited from Wisconsin. As granddaughter Lori Way Galloway remembers it:

> Grandma Wong would come out clamming with us, razor clamming. You dig toward razor clams. And they dig away from you. They don't just sit there like steamer clams. Razor clams have this foot. So they are digging away really fast! You have this big old shovel. . . .
>
> I remember that Grandma would wear the traditional, the pointed Chinese cap, for shade. I was really little, probably five or six. I was really scared because you see in the cartoons that the clams come up and bite on your fingers. But Grandma would put my hand down to show me how to catch the clams. She just loved it. She was so happy clamming with us! Being at the ocean.
>
> She had all this joy, I think, for a lot of things. This joy is about harvesting your own food. We would cook it up and fry it up. You can tell from all of these stories that food is so important in our family!

After her mother's death in 1978, Helen's letters began to convey a deep well of sadness that she had carried since childhood. She had feelings of loneliness in the empty nest. She felt melancholy while Jim was away meeting professional obligations and seeking a different job. He departed for a new position at Texas A&M University Medical School where Helen joined him in 1982. In College Station she missed her friends and life in Pullman and fell into a depression from which she could not emerge. Helen committed suicide in early November 1984, leaving a widower, three heartbroken children on the verge of adulthood, and devastated siblings. At her funeral, Jim Way began his moving eulogy by thanking the Wong family and their friends "for creating an environment to nurture the blossoming of my lovely, elegant lady." He had brought his wife's body back to Beloit and said when they drove into Wisconsin, "there suddenly was a crescendo of thunder and lightning, accompanied by a crashing downpour of rain. It appeared as if heaven and earth were wailing in remorse at the demise of my beloved." Jim also spoke of a six-month-long depression and Helen's request, just two months earlier, that Jim read the following poem by Percy Bysshe Shelley.

> First die our pleasures, and then our hopes, and then our fears.
> When they are all dead, then our debt is due.
> Dust claims dust, and we die too.

Helen Way was buried next to her mother in East Lawn Cemetery in Beloit.

Despite her feelings of deep sadness, it is clear that Helen was immensely proud of her children, Lani, Jon, and Lori; pride born in their personalities, actions, and accomplishments. They, in turn, loved her. Her children learned a love of travel, an appreciation of family and food, and a love of design. They studied the Mandarin language and traveled widely in Taiwan and mainland China.

Family, Medicine, and Physical Activity: Harry

One of Harry's earliest memories of his dad, Charles Wong, was crowding into the family Ford for a Sunday drive. Charles would sleep in while the children went to church; after church their dad would crank up the car and take them out for ice cream or watermelon or some other treat. Harry would have been the youngest of the five older siblings allowed to go along, and he remembers the car being piled high with kids. Harry adored his mother "who did everything for her children." At age five, Harry's bed was located in the hallway near the only bathroom in the house. From this spot he heard a lot of the traffic in the house at night. After his dad's murder, five-year-old Harry remembers hearing his mother cry herself to sleep every night, her grief and suffering of grave concern to all of the children.

Harry (Wong Gim Chow) grew into a fun-loving kid, one who pushed boundaries as he grew. He was the black sheep, the risk-taker who explored new things, the one who would go a little farther than their mother sanctioned and stay out a little too late. He and his friends used to play in a wild, wooded area on the far side of the golf course in Beloit, about a mile from their house on Lincoln Avenue. For that, he remembers Yee Shee "often" taking a branch off the tree to discipline him, though he is quick to explain that she was just trying to keep him in line. Other habits of Harry's would concern her more as he got older.

Harry displayed strong leadership skills in high school. In addition to being elected "most likely to succeed" and "busiest senior boy," Harry was elected class president in his junior and senior years in high school. His popularity in those elections is one reason he says racial discrimination by other kids was a minor issue that didn't concern him. A memorable accomplishment from high school was organizing students to help the school move from its location downtown on West Grand over to the new west riverside location on 4th Street.

Like the others, Harry started working at a very young age and worked his way through university. Most of the money Harry earned went to Yee Shee

Harry Wong, Beloit Memorial
High School, 1951. (Harry Wong)

for household expenses. She allowed the kids to keep about 10 percent of what they earned, an amount that shifted in their favor when they finished high school. Harry started out picking strawberries at a little farm out on Madison Road, where they paid the ten-year-old five cents for a small box of strawberries. More than the money he brought home, the family appreciated that he brought a box of the best berries home every day that he worked. When he was a little older, he delivered papers and then worked construction in his mid-teens, but his most lucrative job was at a factory in Beloit's booming industrial economy.

Harry's future brother-in-law, Elwood Scholz, helped him get a unionized job at Fairbanks, Morse and Company as a high schooler. At the interview, the sixteen-year-old asked for a job where he could earn the most money, and they put him in the foundry with opportunities to earn time and a half on Sundays and holidays. The foundry was hot, dirty, and dusty; it would take weeks after leaving the job each summer for his body to expel the filth. The job changed his life in many ways; most immediately, he got to know the boys and men he worked with, all of them Black American. He got along well with his coworkers. In his junior year of high school, the boys he worked with who were high school wrestlers, J. D. Hoskins and Hickey Edwards, convinced Harry to try wrestling. After work the guys would invite him to drink beer at a Turtle Creek bar "where whites didn't enter."[23]

Harry's opportunity to work at Fairbanks could be analyzed in a number of ways. Since Harry was non-white, it makes sense that he would be given a job among other non-whites in the 1950s industrial economy, fitting a narrative of the existence of jobs for whites and jobs for non-whites. Indeed, starting in the World War I era and continuing into the 1960s, the foundry was where most Black men worked at Fairbanks.[24] In nearby Milwaukee, industries had relegated African American men to jobs at the bottom of the wage scale since the early twentieth century. Discrimination in access to higher wage jobs and equal pay in defense industries only eased in 1943 after Black activists won access to the Fair Employment Practices Committee.[25] Though gains were made, Black workers still faced considerable discrimination in employment in the postwar era. Yet Harry Wong does not view the job in that way. Harry saw the Fairbanks job as an opportunity to make a good, unionized wage during high school and college and to make friends across color lines in high school; friendships that expanded his athletic opportunities and civic role—he was elected president of his class in junior and senior year.[26]

Yee Shee was quite concerned about Harry's drinking habit. She herself did not drink alcohol, and she was concerned when any of her sons came home drunk.[27] One of her most memorable rebukes, used sparingly, was that Harry would "grow up like the man who killed [his] father." Near the end of his time at Fairbanks, Harry nearly lost his hand in an industrial accident. Hungover from the previous night out drinking with friends, his reflexes were off. He was pulling a railcar full of scrap metal with a winch when his gloved hand got caught between the drum of the winch and the rope pulling it. Worse, the winch controls were out of reach, so to prevent an even more catastrophic outcome, for several minutes Harry had to run around the machine, jumping over the rope until someone noticed he was in crisis and came to turn off the machine. He was transported immediately to the emergency room; his family doctor, general practitioner Dr. Smith, found a disarticulated middle and ring finger, and he repaired lacerations to two other digits and a tendon. Miraculously, Harry's hand has been functional ever since.

A surprising outcome of the accident was that the nearly $900 that Harry received in workmen's compensation gave him funds to study at the University of Wisconsin–Madison. In 1951, George and Gim were finishing their engineering degrees, and Helen was also an undergraduate student there. Harry began in the metallurgical engineering program, to which he won a scholarship, but he had harbored an interest in medicine since his industrial accident. He humorously related in an interview that both older brothers agreed to help him pay for medical school if he got in. As soon as the medical school accepted him, they both informed him that they would be married shortly and could no longer help! Harry shifted to pre-med in his third year of college, and he paid for med school by working as an orderly at the Beloit Hospital, working night shifts on top of his normal medical student requirements.

Before marriage, Harry experienced disapproval from his girlfriends' families on racial and ethnic grounds.[28] Harry broke it off with his first serious

Harry Wong anesthesia residency, Madison, Wisconsin, 1960. (Harry Wong)

girlfriend, a white girl he dated in college, whose interest in marrying him, and pressure to do so quickly, was not matched by her parents' interest in him. Race was an issue in that case, though ethnicity mattered in his initial rejection by the Japanese American family of the woman who would become his wife.[29] Harry met Jean, a dietician in training, on the first day of her orientation at the University of Wisconsin. He tracked the beautiful and confident girl from the moment she walked into the lecture hall, late, and took a seat in the front row, right beneath the dean who was giving the orientation speech. He watched in admiration as Jean fell sound asleep during the presentation.[30] Harry was smitten by the shy but intriguing young woman. The fact that she was already engaged to a man back in Hawaii proved a challenge that Harry surmounted when they got to know each other. Originally from Kapaʻa, on the island of Kauai, Jean had been elected national 4-H representative from Hawaii. In that role she had traveled to Washington,

DC, and presented President Harry Truman with a lei (which she put around his arm, since the Secret Service would not allow her to put it around his neck). But Jean's parents were so concerned about the match that it took them ten weeks to reply to Harry's carefully worded letter of request for their permission to marry her. Yee Shee, who had just returned from Hong Kong in 1958 when Harry introduced her to Jean, was not pleased either, at first, but eventually the two became very good friends.

Harry marks getting married and raising a family as his life's greatest joy and personal accomplishment. In June 1958 Harry and Jean were married at the West Side Presbyterian Church in Beloit. Harry and Jean wasted no time starting a family. The first of Harry and Jean's four children, Jeffrey, was born in January 1961, while Harry was completing his anesthesiology residency in Madison. The other three children, Stacey, Daphne, and Steven, were born in Salt Lake City. While Jean was expecting Stacey and Harry was starting his career, he faced the loss of vision in one of his eyes. At age twenty-nine he developed a blood clot in his eye that could have resulted in pulmonary emboli. Specialists in Denver and Boston said Harry had no chance of

Janet Nakahiro, Jean, Steven and Harry, Jeffrey, Stacey, and Daphne Wong in Hawaii, 1965. (David Palmer)

recovering his vision in that eye. Harry struggled with this issue for years: a loss of depth perception might have ended his medical career. He was unable to play tennis, drive, or even do household tasks like pouring milk. Over time, he learned to adapt to the problem and eventually overcame it.

In adulthood, an old pattern re-emerged when Harry found himself periodically drinking to excess. At one memorable family reunion, his older brothers were sent to find Harry, and they found him at a bar in Beloit with old friends. The episode embarrassed Jean in front of the family. She was the one, in the end, who straightened Harry out once and for all. After that episode, Harry always limited himself to one or two drinks over the course of an evening, and he never got drunk again.

Harry experienced racial discrimination embedded in the law in Salt Lake City. When Harry and Jean moved to Salt Lake City with baby Jeff after medical school, they were not able to buy a house in the neighborhood they desired, the East Bench of the Avenues. The city's restrictive covenants had prevented non-whites from buying property in particular areas since the 1920s. Passage of the Civil Rights Act of 1964 immediately allowed Harry and Jean to buy the house they wanted.[31]

Harry's career in Salt Lake City involved three phases: practice, entrepreneurship, and teaching in the clinical field of anesthesiology. When Harry was studying at the University of Wisconsin–Madison, his mentor, Dr. Scott Smith, recruited him to join his practice in Salt Lake City. The University of Wisconsin had been the first medical school to make anesthesiology a specialty in 1926, and it was "the home for anesthesiology" in the late 1950s. Harry practiced as a cardiac anesthesiologist in Salt Lake City between 1961 and 1975. For fifteen years, Harry contributed to improvements in surgical outcomes, especially in cardiac surgery. The practice of anesthesiology made advances in the postwar era. In the World War II era, the mortality rate for that field was nearly 40 percent—that is to say, four out of every ten patients who experienced open heart surgery died. In a short period of time, medical teams brought the mortality rate of that particular type of surgery to less than 4 percent. Technical advances in anesthesiology in the 1960s increased the safety for high-risk patients to tolerate surgical procedures of increasing complexity, such as heart surgeries and heart–lung bypass surgeries.[32]

In the second phase of his career, Harry opened an ambulatory surgical facility, the first in the state of Utah. One of the problems with the Medicare Law in 1965 was that it allowed payment to any medical provider without question. This allowed access to medical care, because it was now feasible to surgically repair fractures in older Americans—such as a broken hip—that had previously been accepted as a natural part of old age that often led to death. But the legislative change also escalated medical costs dramatically. In addition to appropriate increases due to expanded access, the lack of oversight led some to take advantage of the program, such as adult children who admitted elderly parents to a hospital at government expense while they went on vacation. In 1976 Harry and two partners, Dr. John Adair and Dr. Wallace Ring, opened the first freestanding surgical center in Salt Lake City where patients could be treated for surgery on an outpatient basis.[33] Some health insurers charged that medical doctors who owned surgical facilities and conducted surgery had a conflict of interest. However, Harry and partners avoided that potential conflict because, as anesthesiologists, they themselves did not operate. Their focus was on improving the quality and efficiency of surgical care while reducing costs to the health care system. At its peak, the facility included a staff of more than two hundred physicians from every hospital in the community. Harry and his partners sold the practice in 1988.

In the latter part of his career, Harry brought his expertise to the clinical classroom. He taught full-time at the University of Utah Medical School from 1988 to 1995, training medical students, nursing students, and emergency medical technicians (EMTs). Harry was gratified to hear from practitioners in the following decades that they had saved lives using the skills he'd taught them, especially airway management—how to intubate a patient—and emergency resuscitation. Ten years later, the Department of Anesthesiology at the University of Utah Medical School honored him by establishing the Harry C. Wong Presidential Endowed Chair in Anesthesiology.

In recognition of his active participation in the profession, Harry received the Distinguished Service Award from the Society for Ambulatory Anesthesia, having been active in the society throughout his career and served as president. He also served on the Board of Directors of the American Society

Harry and Jean Wong with their extended family, 2018. (Harry Wong)

of Anesthesiologists in Chicago for nine years. After retirement, Harry provided service pro bono to indigent children in need of anesthesiology care while in surgery.

At almost ninety years old, Harry calls physical activity the "single most important factor for longevity." Always athletic, Harry played tennis from junior high school for the rest of his life. He also played golf, fished, and skied for decades. Although Jean had always danced, she convinced Harry to take lessons in his fifties, in advance of daughter Stacey's wedding in 1987. From that humble beginning, they joined a dance club in Salt Lake City, which provided a new social outlet, new friends, and a great deal of fun for more than thirty years. Participating in sports and physical activity like skiing, tennis, and fishing brought him closer to his children, grandchildren, and other relatives.

Family, Chinese History, and Academia: Frank

Frank Wong's legacy is one of complete devotion to his family and career. His marriage to a Chinese woman and two sons brought him great joy. As an adolescent, Frank (Wong Gim Fe) worked as hard as his siblings in high school and achieved even greater academic success. Frank graduated from Beloit Memorial High School as its valedictorian in 1953, the only one of the high-achieving siblings to do so. He earned a full four-year national scholarship to Harvard University in the pre–Civil Rights era. After earning an MA and then a PhD in Chinese History from the University of Wisconsin–Madison, Frank had a successful academic career first as professor of history and then as dean and provost at several colleges. Although cut short by illness, Frank's peers recognized his noteworthy contributions to diversity in liberal education at the Association of American Colleges and Universities.

Frank exchanged regular letters with his sister Mary for decades, allowing a view of his identity formation, including personality, style, and ambitions, from age twenty onward. He enjoyed a close relationship with all of his siblings, but his relationship with Mary, who was two years younger, was especially loving. When Mary was expecting her first child, Frank sent a little monkey as a fun, auspicious symbol of his hopes for the growing child. "The creation of life is always something grandly mysterious and something to be revered and cherished," he wrote.[34] The letters showed his devotion to her and to their growing extended family.

Frank's unique gifts of insight and self-expression were nurtured early. As an eight-year-old boy he created a daily newspaper on a blackboard in the basement, writing news stories and accompanying them with cartoons. During the war he wrote letters and sent news items and cartoons to his brothers and their friends in the service. Usually found with his nose in a book, his mother frequently scolded Frank to get his chores done. Remarkably, he worked for the *Beloit Daily News* before he was old enough to get a paying job. He offered to keep sports statistics on the highly competitive Beloit College basketball team in the Dolph Stanley years, a team that won its conference several years in a row and participated in the National Invitational Tournament in 1951.

In college, Frank expressed a gulf he felt developing from his mother and older siblings because "my interests and pursuits are so different from theirs." He clarified that he did not want to be alienated from the family, "but neither will I compromise my own views of things in order to remain in their good

graces." Above all, he did not wish to "confine [himself] to family expectations."[35] As he matured, however, his relationships matured as well, and
he eased into an open and loving relationship with family members.[36] He
became one of the most enthusiastic proponents of both the Round Robin
newsletter and of regular family reunions.

Frank married Cynthia Ssu-ying Tsao (a.k.a. Cao), whom he met in Taiwan in 1964 when he was there to study the Chinese language at the Stanford Hoover Institute, located at Taiwan National University.[37] Though Frank
used to joke that he "picked her up at a bus stop," Cynthia remembers he
approached her but she only spoke to him after a proper introduction from
his Chinese teacher and landlord, Mrs. Yeh, to her father, General Cao.[38]

Frank and Cynthia
Wong wedding
portrait, 1967.
(Fung Scholz)

Cynthia had been born on the mainland and evacuated to Taiwan with the nationalist army at age three (with her mother and three siblings) in 1949. Cynthia and Frank's dates included attending Pekinese operas, Chinese art museums, the botanical gardens, and the National Palace Museum.[39] Nearly sixty years later, speaking about the way she had been introduced to history, to politics, and to reading widely, Cynthia said about Frank that "he was the best thing to happen in my life."[40] After they wed, Frank reported to Mary they were "very much in love," that Cynthia had "impeccable taste," and that she had "infused his life with beauty."[41] Even before they married in Summer 1967, Frank clearly loved Cynthia's strength, which he associated with her Chinese identity: "She is still quiet, coy in her clever, indirect way. . . . She has the appearance of delicacy and fragility, but occasionally I see flashes of that strong-mindedness which most Chinese women have."[42]

Frank adored children, and none more than his own. He was endeared to many of his nieces and nephews, and frequently mentioned them in his letters to Mary. At one point, Frank reported with amusement that his five-year-old niece, Lani, determined that her Aunt Mary and Uncle David did not have children because their car was too small to carry kids.[43] For their part, Frank and Cynthia tried for years to conceive a child, and to adopt a child from Taiwan, to no avail. Frank worried that they would not be able to have children, and that if they did, he would be too old to be a good father.[44] He worried about the guilt and sadness the couple felt. After many anxious years, the births of his two sons were especially joyous. In November 1975 Cynthia gave birth to their first son, Christopher. Frank told Mary he had spent most of his Christmas vacation in 1975–76 playing with Christopher and caring for him: "I bathe him, change him, and rock him to sleep. What fun! It makes all the difference in the world to have a child."[45] Three years later, Timothy's birth added to the family's joy. The difficulty Frank experienced creating the family he desired contrasted with the ease of his path to professional success.

At only twenty-eight years old, Frank was offered "a plum of a position" as Assistant Professor of Asian History at Antioch College in Springfield, Ohio, in 1963. The job—to teach full-time and procure Asian materials for the college's library—paid $7,000 per year. He was delighted that the college had grants to fund travel to Asia. From the start, Frank had confidence toward his chosen profession; he was selected from among twenty-five candidates, he told Mary, because he had "more breadth of vision" than the other top candidates.[46] That certainly played out. His class on the history of the People's Republic of China was immensely popular, attracting more than seventy students one quarter it was offered.[47] He published in highly regarded journals. After only four years, he was a tenured chair of Antioch's history department, and in 1975 the college offered him the position of Academic Dean and Deputy Chancellor.[48]

Frank's letters depict the changing culture and foreign policy of the United States during the 1960s and 1970s. He described the discotheque that he visited with a girlfriend, Joy, in 1964, where they danced "the surf, the frug,

Cynthia, Frank, Timothy, and Christopher Wong, 1982. (David Palmer)

and the bug." Later allusions are darker, beginning with the tumult of dealing with "student radical revolutionaries" at Antioch in 1967, "frighteningly
freaky" San Francisco in 1971, his ongoing dismay at Richard Nixon's presi-
dency, and more violence—and drugs—on campus in the fall of 1972.[49]
Frank opined that fear of leftist activism drove middle America into the
arms of the Nixon administration.[50] Letters mention gas rationing after the
OPEC oil price shock of 1973 and the Watergate hearings in Congress. "Nixon
and Watergate are almost too much to be believed," he fumed.[51] Frank would
bring his college students to participate in one of the era's most significant
historical changes, the opening of China to the West.

Frank brought Antioch students into China in 1974, on one of the first
academic exchanges with an American institution. Their visit followed President Nixon's official visit by two years, and China was anxious to build on
that diplomatic success. In 1974 Frank entered China via Canada, with one
other professor and eight students. The college had been introduced to Chinese officials through Lois Snow, widow of Edgar Snow, whose daughter
was attending Antioch College.[52] Snow, the author of *Red Star Over China*
(1937), lived in China for more than a decade, beginning in 1929. He was
the first Western journalist to give a full account of the Chinese Revolution
(and Japanese excesses during occupation in World War II), using personal
interviews with Mao Zedong and Zhou Enlai. At the time of Frank's trip,
China was in the throes of the Cultural Revolution, which lasted for two
more years. The extent of the suffering of many Chinese was still unknown
to Frank, although he did meet with his cousin and family in Beijing while
he was there.[53] Frank's reports to Mary indicated great enthusiasm by the
Chinese historian and careful orchestration of the trip by the Chinese government: "We are being treated like honored guests. Every day brings new
and exciting experiences. Don't believe what you read in the newspapers.
Peking is quiet and relaxed. The historical treasures are infinite here. Our
only problem has been eating too much and sleeping too little."[54] If he did
not yet know how the Cultural Revolution had affected his cousins, Frank
did understand the unfolding politics in Beijing, thanks to his training as a
modern Chinese historian. In 1965 he defended his dissertation at the University of Wisconsin–Madison on the reform efforts of a renowned Chinese

scholar from Guangdong province, Liang Qichao, who urged reform of the Qing Dynasty in the early twentieth century. The dissertation focused on the conflict between Confucian and Constitutional politics.[55] Frank focused on U.S.–Chinese relations after his graduate work. In 1967 he met with Chinese refugee students in Hong Kong. He expressed surprise that Chinese youth had ruptured an understanding of their own upbringings with traditional Chinese culture. "They have Chinese family traditions," but they "seem almost completely cut off from traditional Chinese culture."[56] Frank wrote an exceptional review of recent works on China, published in 1969, that presciently called for a complete reconception of U.S. relations with China.[57] That relationship was fundamentally altered in the following years, guided by U.S. Secretary of State Henry Kissinger.[58] Frank understood China, attributing the rise of hardliner Lin Biao and the creation of the Red Guards as a means of reining in independent—and more moderate—Communist Party leaders.[59]

Several aspects of Frank's identity came together in his next position, as Dean and, a year later, Provost and Vice President of Beloit College, back in his hometown in Wisconsin. Founded by early settlers from the East Coast, the college was the oldest in Wisconsin. This was the college Frank had compiled statistics for as a young boy, and two of his brothers (Gim and George) attended the college for a short time. Its history of supporting missionary work in China and welcoming Chinese students went back to the turn of the century, although the Chinese Revolution had ended exchanges. Resuming an exchange program in China was one of Frank's commitments as he took the position. He traveled to Shanghai in 1984 to organize an exchange with Fudan University, a program that lasted until 2005.[60] His experiences in China in the 1970s and 1980s allowed his understanding of its history to develop, as his later scholarship shows.[61]

Given his academic training and his experiences at Antioch, Frank sowed the seeds for an Asian Studies program that continues to thrive at Beloit College.[62] He started a summer language program that included Chinese and Japanese language and literature in 1983, and in 1986 the college hired John Rapp, a political science professor who specialized in Chinese politics and comparative communist systems.[63] Given that the 1980s were lean years at the college, Frank stretched his funds by hiring people in half-time positions and sought funding from sources in the community, including from another Chinese immigrant family in Beloit, the Nies.[64] The family was ready to leave Beloit, however, due to Cynthia's feeling of isolation from a Chinese community and the fact that Christopher experienced racism in the Beloit schools. They welcomed the return to California where Christopher and Timothy "could get to know their peers."[65]

At the University of Redlands in California, Frank served as Dean and later Provost and Vice President for Academic Affairs.[66] When he left that position, due to his illness, President Appleton credited him with having improved the quality of the university while reestablishing its financial stability. The president also recognized Frank's role in launching an Environmental Studies program at the university. About Frank, President Appleton said, "He is a reflective and humane person committed above all else to the values of community, intellectual inquiry, and justice. He wrestles with the challenge of fostering community while acknowledging the realities of diversity."[67]

In the early 1990s, Frank was a leading advocate of diversity on college campuses. He gave addresses and published articles on the issue, which remains a central concern of college and university administrators. Frank argued that intellectual diversity in the academy is a manifestation of cultural diversity and, as such, is "essential to the truth." He hinged his argument on tradition: the Western intellectual tradition welcomed Socratic dialogue. "We believe that if different points of view are expressed, and if these points of view critically engage each other, then a more refined truth will emerge."

There was a mistaken idea, Frank said, that "cultural diversity somehow conflicts with the core values of Western civilization." The problem was that the discussion tended to be dominated by two groups—those on the left, "who believe tradition is unremittingly hostile to multicultural inclusion" and needs to be undermined, and those on the right, who believe that women's studies, ethnic studies, or non-Western studies pose a threat to the fortress of Western civilization and must be denied entry to it. Western civilization had always embraced diversity as an essential condition of the search for truth. "It is precisely for these traditional reasons that we should welcome rather than disdain the new thinking embodied in women's studies, ethnic studies, and non-Western studies."[68] As late as 2011, the American Association of Colleges and Universities (AACU) President Carol Geary Schneider lauded Frank and cited his foundational work in cultivating civic discourse, fostering social justice, and improving race relations.[69]

From his understanding of diversity emerged another significant professional accomplishment, Frank's intellectual leadership in founding an association of professional colleges and universities.[70] What were known as "comprehensive colleges and universities," these midsize schools incorporated elements of two institutional paradigms, liberal arts institutions and research universities. Yet from his experience at the University of Redlands as it compared itself to Stanford University and to the Claremont Colleges, Wong noted, comprehensive institutions seemed to be apologetic about their "disreputable origins." In a 1990 address that puzzled out the problem, Wong noted that the prevailing higher education models came out of two ethnic traditions, English liberal arts and German universities. Each tradition has its strengths. Liberal arts colleges offer personal teaching of "traditional knowledge" in an intellectual community and the personal development of students via their courses, residential life, and extracurricular activities. These institutions, Wong noted, laud the joy of learning for its own sake but disparage applied professional knowledge. By contrast, professionalism and graduate education thrive in autonomous communities at research universities, but in their quest to produce major advances in knowledge and Nobel laureates, these institutions ignore the broad education and character development of the undergraduate. Comprehensive universities are the ugly duckling, Wong argued, whose mixed origins seek to "wrestle with the fundamental, unresolved contradictions in American higher education that are the dual inheritance of the English and Germanic traditions."[71] Frank suggested midsize comprehensive universities restructure to reconcile the strengths of the two types of institution, to hire faculty who would translate "new research of other scholars into a more integrated vision of learning that embodies deliberately humane purpose" into teaching that would "instill a zest for learning into professional training and practical knowledge." This solution would enable the comprehensive universities' search for identity to become a search of discovery and might allow "a fairytale ending," that "the ugly duckling would become the beautiful swan."

Wong's essay had a dramatic impact for a group of deans and provosts of midsize colleges that began to gather in 1988 to discuss an organization for the roughly six hundred comprehensive institutions. Every summer about a dozen administrators would get together to discuss the qualities of their institutions, leading to the Wingspread Conference, held at the Johnson Foundation in Wisconsin, where faculty, dean/provosts, and presidents from fourteen institutions gathered. Two leading figures of higher education attended the conference, Ernest Boyer, President of the Carnegie Foundation for the Advancement of Teaching at Princeton University, and Alexander Aston, the "best known higher education statistician" from the UCLA Higher Education Research Institute.[72] At the conference, the group named itself the New American Colleges (NAC), a name coined by Frank Wong. In April 1995 Boyer invited the group to the Carnegie offices at Princeton to formally announce the creation of the new organization, the Association of New American Colleges and Universities. The creation of this organization was one of Frank's proudest professional accomplishments. At their ten-year anniversary, the NAC recognized Frank Wong's contributions as one of their founding figures.

Larger national academic organizations recognized Frank Wong for his work. He was a consultant to the Ford Foundation. He was a member of the Board of Directors of the AACU.[73] In January 1995 the AACU held a special program to honor Frank's work and announced an award for his record of "Distinguished Intellectual Leadership in advancing a vision and practice for American Liberal Education that deepen and broaden the academy's commitment to truth, justice, public engagement and the expansion of our capacities as an inclusive, multicultural and self-reflective democracy."[74] Already ill with the cancer that would claim his life in April, Frank attended the conference, spoke at it, and received the honor of a standing ovation by the fifteen hundred attendees who had come in his honor.[75]

Family, Education, and History: Mary

The youngest of the siblings, Mary Wong (Wong Fung Me), grew up an extrovert who, in later years, devoted herself to preserving the memory of her family. Mary felt like her older siblings Gim and Fung had raised her. The brothers who were closer in age teased her, and she felt, until senior high school, that she was a mere tagalong to her sister Helen. After her father's death, when Mary was just seventeen months old, it was Gim who stood in her father's place, and even asked if she would object to his getting married before she left for college.[76] And Fung, who was eleven years older than Mary and had chosen her English name at birth, had taken her everywhere after their father's death.[77]

Mary describes a very happy childhood imbued with both American and traditional Chinese values. She played hide-and-seek and kick the can in the street with her siblings and friends, and she played on the Royce School summer recreation baseball team that won the city tournament the summer she played. "So I grew up pretty much like everyone else," she said. A neighbor, Fanchon Rosenblatt, invited Mary in to listen to her play the piano, an invitation that led Fung to purchase a used piano and lessons for Mary. Mary learned Chinese values at home that carried her into adulthood. Her mother fostered strong relationships among the children. Although she did not work outside the home, they saw her constantly busy. She arose every morning before dawn to stoke the coal fire. She cooked every meal and made all of their clothing. Daily laundry required washing, hanging dry, and ironing. Each of the daughters helped with these tasks as they became old enough, and Mary remembers doing the banking and shopping with her mother from a young age. Most importantly, Yee Shee encouraged her children to do their best in every endeavor in order to bring honor to the family.

With this strong sense of self, Mary was not bothered by feelings of racial difference in childhood. She found it curious that her mother instructed her as a kindergartner to remember to say she was Chinese, not Japanese, but she did not understand until much later when she became close friends with a Japanese American woman that it was because the United States was allied with China and at war with Japan in World War II. Mary said racial

Mary Wong in Miss McKinley's first grade class at Royce School, 1943. (David Palmer)

taunts by neighborhood kids did not bother her because the family was so well-established and respected. She walked in the path that her siblings had forged.

Mary was a high-achieving high school student who was engaged in many extracurricular activities. She followed the examples of her siblings, especially those closest in age. Like Harry and Frank, she was elected to a leadership role in student government. Like Gim, she was editor of the school year-book; like Fung, she was elected to the National Honor Society; like George, she volunteered for the Red Cross; and like Helen, she played in the band. Her peers voted her "most likely to succeed" (as they had done for Harry and Frank) and "busiest senior girl."

Of all the siblings, Mary credits the neighbors and community the most in her upbringing. "The neighborhood supported all of us, me especially," Mary says. While her mother was grieving her father's death when Mary was still a baby, she lived with close family friends from the same block, Avis

Mary Wong in
Beloit Memorial
High School band
uniform, 1953.
(David Palmer)

Bord and her children. Mary herself did not know about the arrangement
until her brother Gim's funeral in 1991. Avis's daughters, Gloria and Beth,
told Mary that the neighbors heard Yee Shee's wailing at night since her
father had died in summertime, when the windows were always open. Avis
Bord, whose husband had left the family, took baby Mary in for as long as
three and a half or four months. This generous act drew the families close
and the Bords became "like extended family."[78]

Mary attributes her early paid work to neighbors' desire to help her family. She started out as a babysitter for neighborhood children; as a very
young child the neighbors, Ann and Arthur Loft, invited her to play with
their baby, Barbara. Mary walked Barbara to school when she started kindergarten and later worked for Arthur Loft. At age thirteen, a memorable
summer job was being a full-time caregiver for her dentist's son. For ten dollars a week, Mary worked eight to five, dressing and caring for the baby,

cleaning, and hanging laundry in the yard. Another family, upon hearing the amount of work required of her for this low weekly wage, told her to request a raise to twelve dollars a week, which she successfully negotiated. At fifteen, Mary got a job as a soda jerk at Bach Drugstore on the corner where West Grand, 8th Street, and Brooks Street meet, and she worked there through high school. By the time she left that job, she also acted as an assistant to the pharmacist, Merritt Bach, who wrote a letter recommending her for college scholarships.

Neighbors, employers, and teachers understood the precarious position of Yee Shee and her children after they lost their primary breadwinner. With no disrespect to the family, adults around the Wong family stepped up to offer guidance and support. Mary says she learned the fundamentals of good work habits at the drugstore. When it was busy, you pitched in however you could, and when it was slow you took up tasks like cleaning and planning for the next rush. Another lesson was in tolerance. There was an elderly couple who frequented the pharmacy, one of whom (the woman) had dementia. Her husband had an agreement with the pharmacy personnel that his wife could put things in a bag that they would take home. Later, her husband would bring the items back, and they would be returned to the shelf. With no ugly confrontation between workers and customers, the storeowner taught his young employee how a community looks out for its most vulnerable members.

The boss's generosity extended to meeting the needs of the poor. If a customer came in for medications or any other item but was unable to pay for them at that moment, the pharmacy owner would write it down on a slip of paper and allow the customer to pay up later when they could afford it. Similarly, when the Wongs were barely making ends meet in the late 1930s and early 1940s, the butcher at the Bonnie Bee market saved bones and meat scraps for Yee Shee to use in soups. These are the sorts of community-strengthening accommodations possible with locally owned stores. These are the small acts of kindness Beloit residents extended to less fortunate neighbors.

Beyond the immediate neighborhood, Mary benefited from a commitment to a strong city and state community. One of the reasons she played the French horn in high school was that a citywide music program tested children for musical abilities and funneled them into free lessons with free instruments. Afterschool activities at the high school, such as student government, never involved extra fees. Teachers mentored the children in ways that extended far beyond the high school years. Mary and her husband kept in touch with the National Honor Society advisor and his wife, Lloyd and Peggy Page, for more than fifty-five years.

Mary was the fifth Wong to attend the state flagship university. Like the others, generous scholarships made her attendance possible. She earned a "special racial background" scholarship for students who were non-white who planned to attend the University of Wisconsin–Madison. Mary made ends meet in other ways, too, by working on campus and back in Beloit at Chapman's, a clothing store owned by her neighbor Arthur Loft, during breaks; by living in a lower-cost cooperative dormitory, Zoe Bayliss; and by being in the Integrated Liberal Studies Program and working part-time for a chemistry professor.[79] She graduated with honors with a degree in elementary education in 1959.

Mary met her future spouse, David Palmer, in the high school band. Their dates mirrored American conventions at the time, with David walking Mary home after her shift at the drugstore or going for a hamburger to the High C in South Beloit. Like most of her siblings, Mary faced rejection by David's parents, specifically his mother, who said her concern was for the mixed-race children. The two made an effort to split up and date other people in college, but their relationship endured, and they married June 11, 1959, at First Presbyterian Church in Beloit. After college, Mary taught school in Madison while David continued in graduate school. He earned a PhD in nuclear physics from the University of Wisconsin–Madison in 1965.

Mary came of age in an era when women's gender role expectations had eased in some ways but still funneled them into certain studies and careers. Unthinkable in America before the 1930s, Mary wore pants and played sports in the 1940s. She took mainly the same high school coursework as her male peers, and she was considered for college scholarships based on merit. Yet like other young women who graduated from high school in the 1950s, her gender shaped her college major and professional choices. Whereas the war had offered greater opportunities for women, in the 1950s domestic ideology and American Cold War concerns reinforced each other to limit women's professional choices.[80] While her brothers envisioned careers such as engineer, medical doctor, and academic scholar, these fields were simply not open to women before the 1970s. Her sisters had thrived in the parts of the medical field open to women, and Mary decided she would go into education because she "always liked kids and at that time teachers were in great need." Her field of concentration was social sciences and, as a backup, she also studied library science for flexibility in the job market while David was in graduate school. Partly signaling the lesser status of women's careers, Mary forgot to mention in her interview that she had won accolades as a student at the University of Wisconsin. She had been elected to two education honor societies: Pi Lambda Theta and Phi Kappa Phi. She was tapped for the very selective Mortar Board in her junior year of college, which thrilled her because her older sister, Helen, had also been tapped.[81]

Mary's leadership ability won recognition beyond the university classroom. She was selected for the King Gustav Christian Award for Interfaith

Mary Wong in news clipping about Youth Conference from *Beloit Daily News*, 1961. (Mary Wong Palmer)

Contributions. She also served on a panel for interracial, interfaith education that focused on similarities among people rather than their differences.[82] Her most singular honor was selection to serve, first, on the Governor's State Youth Committee and then to represent the state at a national conference.[83] In 1960 Mary was selected to be in the group that represented the State of Wisconsin at the White House Conference on Children and Youth, where she heard President Eisenhower speak.[84]

Mary's career in education was based on an idealistic vision of the importance of imparting values to the next generation and the personal belief that income and race did not matter in school settings. In college at the University of Wisconsin–Madison she observed an educator at Franklin School, on Lake Shore Drive in Madison. Early idealism attracted her to this school, where she believed she could make a difference. Franklin had the highest proportion of kids in the Madison School District whose parents received federal Aid to Dependent Children support. The principal at Franklin School thought highly of her work and hired her in 1959, at $4,200 a year, to start her career there as a fourth-grade teacher. Mary was the only teacher of color in the schools she worked in, and she soon met the first Jewish teacher to be hired in the Madison Public Schools, who also started in 1959.[85] Mary experienced the school faculty as "lily white." She felt conflicted at Franklin, where she felt more like a social worker than a teacher. Students who needed extra help came early to school or stayed after every day to work intensively with her. Children with improper winter gear arrived with wet, cold feet so that she felt compelled to bring David's socks to school for them. One parent confronted her about her message to his daughter not to fight back if she were hit by another child, the exact opposite of what he had taught her. Another problem was an "old school" principal who used outdated techniques such as washing children's mouths out with soap for swearing. So Mary transferred to Van Hise, a new school on Madison's West Side, where the children's parents were mainly middle class and employed by the university.

Mary remembers that virtually every teacher was female, and school policies favored single teachers. If a teacher became pregnant she was required to leave her job at three months or as soon as she was "showing." Because of this requirement and anticipating a move and starting a family, Mary resigned from Madison Public Schools in June 1964. She used the time to help David finish his dissertation, after which she accompanied David and their first child, Jimmy, to Brazil for David's postdoctoral research in experimental nuclear physics. Mary's gendered identity expresses itself further in her reasoning to continue her education. Upon their return to Madison for another postdoctoral fellowship, Mary "found herself with the time" to complete a master's degree in education at the University of Wisconsin–Madison and supervise student teachers.

In the expanding 1960s national educational sector, David and Mary's lives changed dramatically as they moved for academic work. David desired to teach at a small liberal arts college, as his father had. He interviewed rather well, and when offered Assistant Professor positions at Carleton College, Pomona College, and Kalamazoo College, he selected Carleton, in Minnesota, rejecting Pomona after a visit there revealed that the heightened air pollution would not be desirable for raising a family. The opening at Carleton was assured for one year, replacing a physicist who was on a leave of absence and not expected to return. When he did return, however, David moved to Kalamazoo College as an Assistant Professor in a newly created position funded for four scientist faculty members by a four-year Sloan Foundation grant that was intended to strengthen science programs at liberal arts colleges. This promised a stable future for the family, and shortly after moving there their second child, Sharon, was born. After four years in Kalamazoo, the college decided it could not continue supporting the four newly hired science faculty, as promised for the Sloan grant, so another means of support had to be found. Mary was devastated to leave Kalamazoo, where she had established such deep roots and friendships, as well as her family in the Midwest. Larger forces were at work that propelled the young family to the West Coast.

In a very difficult economy, with federal funds for science education cut at liberal arts colleges but increased at research institutions, David and Mary floundered for a bit until David was offered a job at University of California, Berkeley to retrain as a medical physicist. In the Cold War period, Berkeley had emerged as the first public university to best Harvard University in

David, Mary, Jim, and Shari Palmer, 1971. (David Palmer)

drawing federal research funds and enjoyed a reputation as "the most productive research faculty in the world . . . particularly in the physical sciences."[86]
The transition was difficult for Mary, who negotiated distance from family
and cultural differences between the Midwest and the West Coast.

Making dear friends and welcoming support from family resolved feelings of alienation. Because of job uncertainties, in the summer of 1973 Mary
sought work at a private clinic for learning disabled children, Reach for Learning, in Mill Valley and later in Berkeley. Grandmother Wong came out for
the summer to care for the children, now four and eight. When she left in the
fall, the family formed an informal babysitting exchange that involved no
money, just time, with friends Naomi and Bill Lidicker and also Birthe and
Jack Kirsch; the wives helped Mary and David out with babysitting when
needed. In exchange, Mary and David babysat the Lidicker kids overnight or
on weekends to allow Naomi and Bill to get away. Mary unexpectedly learned
about Japanese internment as a result of her friendship with Naomi Lidicker,

who was Japanese American. Naomi's family of five had been abruptly taken to an assembly center in Stockton, California, and sent by train to the Rohwer Japanese American Relocation Camp in Arkansas. Though Naomi had not thought of it previously, and had not discussed internment with her friends or family, the friendship allowed the two women to explore the divergent paths their lives took as Asian American women.[87]

Although job opportunities were greater on the West Coast, the Palmers moved back to Wisconsin in 1976. David was offered a position as Medical Physicist in the Department of Nuclear Medicine at the Medical College of Wisconsin. Mary worked as a special ed teacher in the suburban Milwaukee School District of Wauwatosa until she retired in 1994. Living just an hour from her mother and older brothers allowed Mary and her family to be back in close touch with the extended family. One change Mary and David made in their lives in Wauwatosa was to join a church. This helped Mary process the grief she felt after her sister, Helen, died in 1984. They found a community of friends that lasted beyond their move back to California in 2018.

Mary's legacy to her family comes from her deep desire to know her history. She kept letters and cards from Frank, Helen, and others, letters that show deeply honest, supportive relationships. From Frank and Helen, she picked up an interest in family genealogy, and after their deaths, Mary felt a need to fulfill their goal of discovering the Wong family history. Over about a decade, Mary and David traveled all over the country and overseas to piece together the very complicated history of the Wong family with help from Harry and interviews with her other siblings.

The younger Wong siblings had different opportunities than their older siblings, in part because there were fewer familial responsibilities but also because prospects changed for college-bound teens in the United States in the 1950s. With the luxury of knowing their older siblings would stay close to and care for their mother, Helen, Harry, Frank, and Mary were free to take jobs and lead lives outside of the Midwest. They met more Chinese, Chinese Americans, and Asian Americans, and three of the four started families with Asian partners. They expressed the values of service to family by caring for their mother, for each other in times of need, and for their nieces and nephews. Along with their older brother George, Helen, Harry, Frank, and especially Mary sought to understand—and celebrate—how their family had come about, why their parents had chosen Beloit, Wisconsin, and what values and experiences they wished to pass down to the younger generations. The periodic family reunions allow the siblings—and now their children and grandchildren—to connect and celebrate the values and traditions that undergird their experiences.

CHAPTER SIX

Family Reunions

Legacies and Advice for the Next Generations

The most memorable reunion was San Diego in 2005. I was 13. I wanted to stay in Dayton because a musical camp I had gone to had a reunion I wanted to attend. Mom said I couldn't go because of the family reunion. I was so mad but then I had a blast connecting to cousins at the reunion! They became my friends. It was so much fun being able to connect with people with similar experiences as mixed-race persons in the United States.

—Alex Dereix, daughter of Wendy Wong Dereix,
granddaughter of Gim

Age 28, fourth-generation Alexandra (Alex) Dereix has enthusiastically attended every Wong family reunion since the age of 13 when she discovered how fun and valuable it was to connect to her family of cousins who "are spread out across the country and world." Discussions with elders and evening programs at reunions gave her pride in the hard work that her grandparents and great-grandparents did and a desire to "live up to their legacy." For Alex, the legacy is not about attending an Ivy League college or achieving a PhD; what is prioritized in the family, she said, is "trying your hardest and putting in the effort."

Reunions also provide Alex a way to work through issues of identity. Especially in the present era of rampant racial discrimination against Black Americans, Asian Americans, and Latinos, Alex—who points out that her features mark her as ethnically ambiguous—regularly hears micro and macroaggressions against non-whites, including Asians, and often feels the need to "defend her Asian heritage." As a mixed-race person, what box on the census should she check when it comes to race? Should her first-generation American status through her father outweigh her fourth-generation Chinese American status? Scholar Jennifer Ho reveals the tensions for Asian Americans in "choosing which identities, forms of affiliation, and membership in various collectivities one wishes to demonstrate at any given time versus the ways others try to constrain that choice."[1] Ho notes that it is easier to work through the tensions with like-minded peers (or siblings). Like her cousins in the fourth generation, Alex expressed that reunions allowed her to "figure out what it means to be a mixed-race Chinese American in a predominantly white area of the Midwest."[2]

Beyond identity, Alex appreciates how connections to extended family have shaped her career. She recognizes the effort generations before hers made to know extended family. Because she came to know them at reunions, Alex and her boyfriend stopped in Salt Lake City when they were college students on a cross-country trip, stayed with her great-uncle and aunt, Harry and Jean Wong, and connected with their son, Steven Wong. She discussed her hope of attending medical school with them, and Harry read her résumé and gave her advice for her application. Having conducted research on the effects of environmental toxins on children in utero and then studied for a master's degree in public health, Alex is presently in medical school with the hope of becoming an OB-GYN who will influence and promote health among young, poor persons of color. With these ambitions, Alex embodies the hope of her generation, a generation her cousin Tim Rosenwong describes as "the hope for the future of my [mixed-race] son."[3]

Alex's great-grandmother Yee Shee would be delighted to know the reunions continue. Well into her seventies, Yee Shee visited her growing family as they found jobs and established lives in cities beyond the Midwest. Her purpose was to ensure that her children and their children thrived. Jon Way remembers many happy fishing and clamming trips with his grandmother, who relished cooking and eating seafood and spending time with him and his sisters.[4] Yee Shee bonded with the next generation and instilled her love of food and family. Starting in 1957, in order to visit more frequently with extended family, the family began holding a family reunion every five years in Beloit so that the family could gather around her there. As grandson Alan Scholz remembers:

We had a lot of family picnics, the Wongs did. We went to Leeson Park, we went to Rockford, we had picnics all over the place, for thirty, forty people. And everybody would cook foods and bring them but my grandmother was really something. She made all of these baos, we'd call them, and different buns with things in them and a soup called *jook* and another soup that had sweet rice dumplings in it. It was a wonton soup, a chicken soup. But it had these little sweet rice dumplings that I just loved. And I guess the favorite would have been some of the buns she made that had pork filling. I liked everything she cooked.

In holding regular reunions, the Wong family was participating in a time-honored ritual of extended family gatherings to honor a common ancestor and each other.[5] Historian Robert Taylor theorized that family reunions represent an effort to provide stability in an era of profound change. As urbanization and mobility challenged the durability of the rural family unit in the latter part of the nineteenth century, more middle-class American families sought to "summon the wandering tribes" for regular reunions.[6] Taylor linked together the rise in popularity of the American family reunion and the pursuit of genealogy. He argued that in moments of profound social change, families sought to document family traditions in histories and genealogies to provide a reliable record for their descendants of what was done in the past and is being done in the present to prescribe what must be done in the future. Taylor suggested the most important features of family reunions are to identify and mobilize family resources among generations and to offer a platform for counseling younger family members.

If family reunions are quintessentially American, the format of the Wong reunion, with its culmination in a banquet and formal program, also manifests its Chinese roots. Scholars have shown how Chinese immigrants in the United States created a strong network of organized groups—from family associations to benevolent societies—that helped them to form and maintain community.[7] Paul Siu described the significance of the festivals, rites, and ceremonies of the Chinese community in early twentieth-century Chicago. "The most persistently observed" was the clan's commemoration of the spring festival, "a banquet followed by speeches and messages by elder men and celebrities of the clan."[8] In this way, the Wong gatherings represented a hybrid of Chinese ceremony and American family reunion traditions.

The early Wong family reunions, held in the late 1950s, 1960s, and 1970s, are preserved in memory and photographs. Family members fondly remember gatherings at the house on Lincoln Avenue in Beloit, recalling especially the fun they had with cousins, aunts, and uncles and the classic dishes that Grandma would prepare. The only reunion scheduled out of the five-year rotation was when the family gathered to celebrate Yee Shee's eightieth birthday in 1975. After Yee Shee died in 1978, four of the siblings living near Beloit—Gim, George, Fung, and Frank—sponsored a reunion in 1982 that set the tone and program for future reunions. The gathering was a way to come together to remember Yee Shee, to celebrate their Chinese heritage and history, and to

Grandma Yee Shee and her extended family at family reunion, 1968. (Bill Wong)

give their children a chance to meet and get to know cousins who were now located across the country, from Pennsylvania to California. The reunion has become the central means of passing along family wisdom and traditions and of making connections among extended Wong family members.

Family Wisdom and Traditions

The program for the 1982 reunion celebrated the Wong's Chinese American heritage and family traditions. This was what the family recalls as the Year of the Big Box. The reunion took place on the Beloit College campus, where Frank was Vice President of Academic Affairs. All the family gathered around a box and, to the surprise and delight of the children, Frank popped out of it.[9] From that vantage, he delivered a poem that celebrated the family's heritage and history to open the evening's program. The poem captured Frank's witticisms; his gentle ribbing and self-deprecation were also on full display. So, too, were his messages for the next generation. The poem welcomed the guests to the reunion of Yee Shee and Charles's seven children, the "singular seven birds" who were gathered there together with their own children at

Frank Wong popping out of a box at family reunion, 1982. (Lisa Fortsch)

the reunion, "a common nest for birds of a feather." Frank commented on their shared history that this "unusual" family had sprung from "a remarkable mother," and that in spite of the difficulties they had endured while coming of age, the children were "flourishing here" with "personal achievements and honors galore." He humorously described each of his siblings and himself, honoring Fung's maternal input, Helen's thriftiness, and his own devotion to reading. In addition to kindness, thrift, and intellectual pursuit, Frank acknowledged the benefits of marriage. Among their successes, each had a "patient, long-suffering spouse." The poem affirmed Yee Shee's values of family attachment and the twin ethics of outward humility and inward personal achievement and honor.

There is no jack in this box
But rather, quick as a wink,
You find before you, a "collapsible Frank,"
To greet you on this fine occasion
When each and every Wong generation
Celebrates a noble line
That ages well like the best of wine.

Seeded in an ancient land
Flourishing here to beat the band
Roots and trunks and branches more
Personal achievements and honors galore,
Now gathered for this get together
A common nest for birds of a feather.

Let me speak some sundry words
About the singular seven birds
The eldest one, though lacking hair
Has ample waistline with some to spare.
The next in line with great affection
Spoiled the others, each in succession.

Number two son, with temper rare,
Hollywood looks and gorgeous hair.
Second sister with wanderlust
Yet saves every penny, like it's a must.
Third brother, remembered most of all,
He boxed my ears when I was small!
Then yours truly next in line
Reading books too much of the time.
Finally came the baby runt
Of all the jokes she bore the brunt.

This unusual group, this, that, and the other
Could only spring from a remarkable mother.
Now each in their turn have produced their own,
Some of them small, some of them grown
Each with a patient, long-suffering spouse
Who earns the keep or keeps the house.
Now with all pride and pretense shorn
Will for their children, attempt to perform.

The Big Box jest was followed by a song written and performed by Mary and Helen, the "Von Wong Singers." The song threaded melodies from the iconic movie about the Von Trapp Singers, *The Sound of Music*, to playfully describe personalities of the second generation and their spouses. Many jokes were about responsibility avoidance, whether it was George Wong's attempts to avoid mowing the lawn as a teen, Jim Way's tendency to go out for the evening with his brothers, or Marion's regular requests for babysitters. By making light of these tricks, the song asserted the family values of responsibility and commitment.

Sung to the tune of "The Hills Are Alive with the Sound of Music":

Beloit is alive with the sound of children
A song that we've heard for a long, long time . . .

[Spoken]
Like these sounds of children . . .
Mary—crying
Frank—I didn't do it!
Harry—Can I use the car, Dad?
Helen—Now what, Mom?
George—I will mow the lawn tomorrow.
Fung—I don't want any vegetables!
Gim—Will you accept a collect call?
David—It's your turn to feed the dog!
Cynthia—I do not know.
Jean—I'll clean my room tomorrow!
Jim—My brothers are picking me up!
Joyce—It's his turn to do the dishes!
Marion—Can you babysit?

[Sung]
I go to Beloit when my heart is yearning
The memories will last for a thousand years,
Our hearts will be blessed with the sound of children,
And we'll need no more!

The song ended with a heartwarming affirmation of the years of close-knit family relations, sung to the tune of "So Long, Farewell, Auf Wiedersehen, Adieu":

Goodbye, Farewell, Zai Jian, Zai Jian, Good night
We hate to go, but we must say [while exiting]
    Good night—Good night
    Good night—Good night

Ten years later, Frank reprised the Big Box jest a third time with a poem that his son Timothy read at the 1992 reunion. Fourteen-year-old Timothy, the younger of Frank and Cynthia's two boys, was the youngest of the generation that was now coming of age. In addition to reiterating the spirit of the jest, the ballad was an ode to Frank's happiness about the fact that he and Cynthia were now parents and his pleasure at the strength of his relationships with his nieces and nephews.

> Before my dad was a dad
> He often was sad beyond sad
> What he wished he had was some kids

Frank noted how important his nieces' and nephews' reactions had been to him when he performed the ballad ten years earlier.

> A rhyme he read to them all
> To teach them of his generation
> The struggles, the joys, the occasional falls
> An immigrant family's transformation
> In hopes the story would be told
> To serve for many an inspiration.
> . . .
> At the time of each child's belief
> In the wonder and freshness of life
> Their wide-eyed surprise gave relief
> From troubles and trials so rife.

Near the end of the ballad, Frank repeated the educational intent of the Big Box jest and poem, and he closed with an affirmation of regular family reunions to "preserve the family as the center." At the moment that his nieces and nephews were starting families of their own, it was important to remember the need to remain close.

> Preserve the family as the center
> Though life's distraction all would enter
> The box's meaning after all
> To one generation, another's call

The renewal of life is what it means
Even as cloudy as life would seem
At each reunion as we gather
We affirm the need to stay together.

Programs at later reunions repeated reverence for family history and tradition. Shari Palmer and Andy Dimock wrote a play for the 2005 reunion in
San Diego. Fourth-generation Wongs played the roles of Yee Shee, Charles,
their children, and various others. The play is remarkable for its conceptual-
ization of complex history and its historical accuracy. Three scenes portrayed
the arrival and social isolation of Yee Shee in the United States in 1923, Yee
Shee's relationships with neighbors and her decision to remain in the United
States after Charles was killed in 1938, and the children's successes. The scenes
are replete with grace and humor, but they are also instructive.[10] They offer
information without burdening the next generation with exaggerated expectations of achievement. The full play can be found in the Appendix.

Two other notable programs offered family history and tradition: a game
show designed for the 2008 reunion and the 2013 unveiling of the Wong
Genealogy Website. Wendy Dereix, Gim's daughter, wrote the game show
with the goal of "passing on family lore to the second and third generation in
a fun and funny way."[11] Well in advance of the reunion, Wendy sent attention-
grabbing questions, such as "Tell us the funniest joke you've ever played on
your brothers and sisters" to Mary, Harry, George, and Fung so that they
could prepare their responses. Other questions asked about growing up without television or Internet and what it was like to live during World War II.
In her reply to the latter, Mary described how frightening nighttime black-
out drills were for her as a little girl in wartime Beloit. This vivid description
was bound to capture the attention of, and thereby instruct, her great-nieces
and nephews. At the 2013 reunion, Bill Wong presented the online genealogy
he had created. Bill had started gathering information for a book and realized
a website would be the best place to collect and preserve the historical documents from the family members.

Cherie Scholz Baker, Lisa Wong Fortsch, and John and Becky Wong
worked together to create a fund in 2013 that drew on family lore to encourage

additional participation from their own and their children's generations. The fund, "Grandma's Candy Dish," takes donations to offset costs for attendance at the reunions. The year they began it, for example, donations lowered the cost of shared meals over three days to only $35 per person. The explanation of the fund began with the following anecdote:

> Do you remember anxiously going into Grandma's dining room and lifting the top [of Grandma's red metallic candy dish] to find either lemon drops or Hershey Kisses? This was done multiple times during any visit to her house! Along with this memory, we all have so many others from multiple family reunions over the course of the past 40+ years. Grandma was a proud woman, and rightfully so. She instilled in all of us the values and morals we all carry on to the next generation, our children. Hard work, respect, patience, resourcefulness, education, and family, just to name a few. The last one, family, is the focus of this mailing.[12]

Grandma Yee Shee's candy dish with chocolate kisses and lemon drops. (Lisa Fortsch)

As Yee Shee taught them, preparing and eating food is a critically important activity for socializing and acculturation at the reunions. An early "regrets" message from one granddaughter noted her memory of "eating Grandma's Popsicles, eating Grandma's eggrolls, eating Grandma's dim sum, eating Grandma's soup, eating, eating, eating. . . ."[13] In the early reunions, Yee Shee's daughters, daughters-in-law, and grandchildren prepared most of the food consumed over the three or four days. For a picnic, for example, Marion Wong contributed potato salad; Joyce, fruit salad; Fung, tossed salad; and Mary, cookies and brownies. The families would share the cost of the meat they purchased to grill. At the same reunion, grandchildren Wendy Dereix, Lani Way, and Jeff Wong prepared dishes inspired by their grandmother: baked and steamed cha siu bows, wonton soup, egg rolls, barbecue chicken, sliced cucumbers, and pac-man cupcakes. As families dispersed and

**Welcome to San Diego and
The Wong Family Reunion!!!**

Here is a brief rundown of our time together. Feel free
to join us as the mood takes you.

- Thursday evening 6:45 - until we all get tired and go to bed. Meet and Greet. Poolside at the Residence Inn.

- Friday afternoon. Golf. Tee times are 12:00, 12:07 and 12:15 at the Cottonwood Ivanhoe Course. Directions and map included.

- Friday evening. Chinese buffet. 6:00 is when we will begin to gather. It is a buffet so you can wander in at your leisure. Come and go as you please, there are no formal arrangements although those that gather around the same time can try to sit together. It will be held at the Great Moon Buffet. Directions and map included.

- Saturday evening. Wong Family Reunion Dinner. Doors open at 5:00. We hope to begin eating at 6:00. During and following dinner there will be a program (whether it is long or short, we have no idea at this point!) This is being held at the Lisbon Room at the Ramada Inn and Conference Center, right across the street from the Residence Inn.

- There are many things to do in San Diego. The lobby of the Residence Inn has many brochures dealing with various sites and attractions around the San Diego area.

Enjoy! We are happy you are here!

Wong Family Reunion schedule, 2005. (Lisa Fortsch)

the number of attendees grew, it became apparent that food preparation was a task that fell especially hard on the women in whatever family organized the event, and so the family decided to cater more meals during the reunions.

Reunions often featured a Chinese banquet and program. The dishes at local Chinese restaurants will be familiar to Chinese Americans: bird's nest soup, roast duck, sweet and sour fish, squid and vegetables. There were memorable banquets at the New Hong Kong Restaurant in Seattle's Chinatown (2011), the China Palace in Rockton, Illinois (1987), the Great Moon Restaurant in San Diego (2005), the Szechuan Restaurant in Park City, Utah (1992), among other venues. A formal program, a one- or two-hour-long affair, often followed the Chinese banquet.

Connections between Family Members

A second goal of the family reunion was to reconnect with family around special anniversaries, birthdays, and to welcome new spouses. The program for the 1982 reunion encouraged the development of relationships among the third-generation Chinese American family and between members of the second and third generations. In 1982 Yee Shee's twenty-two grandchildren were between ages four and twenty-eight. They needed friends who shared their Chinese American heritage and values. They needed role models and advice about college and career paths. The family provided both.

In the same way that family leadership passed from Charles and Yee Shee to Gim and Fung, and then to the younger siblings, the responsibility for organizing the reunions passed from the second to the third generation. The younger generation stepped up as they approached middle age, with Stacey, Daphne, and Lori organizing the reunion in San Diego in 2005. Organization was always complicated; it required selecting an appropriate site, negotiating rate reductions with a hotel, and finding appropriate activities and venues for attendees, such as golf courses, water parks, concerts, and restaurants. Organization was time-consuming, but it also offered an opportunity to collaborate with cousins and to reach out and get to know the extended family.

The Wongs recognized the benefits of spending time together in smaller numbers. Time and space were reserved at every reunion to socialize. One aspect of the 1982 reunion was a revolving brunch: members of different families would gather at the four hosts' homes for brunch each day. For example, on Monday, Gim and Marion Wong hosted Helen and Jim Way; on Tuesday they hosted Harry and Jean Wong; on Wednesday they hosted Mary and David Palmer and Bill and Ann Wong; and on Thursday they hosted cousins Terry Lee and Bob Wong. The scheduling was set but also flexible enough to be able to add cousins Albert and Kathryn Wong, and Gloria and George Moy to the brunch Frank and Cynthia Wong hosted on Thursday.[14]

Programs planned and unplanned allowed organizers and attendees to get to know each other. Musical numbers required coming together in rehearsal and performance. An evening program the year the reunion was held at Beloit College included a musical interlude by the "in-law band," composed of Marion Wong, Joyce Wong, Jim Way, Jean Wong, Cynthia Wong, and David Palmer, who played pot-cover cymbals, the triangle, washboard, and bugle. In 2011 another group—Pete, Helen, Lani Way, and Chris Wong—came together to play bluegrass music for forty-seven assembled family members.[15] Mary Wong Palmer shared a PowerPoint presentation on the family history and new information on Mong Dee village in China, a result of her trip to China in 2008. Oftentimes there were separate outings for the different generations, such as golf for the elders and a water park for the children and teens. Sometimes the fun was unplanned, such as the water balloon fight for children and adults at the reunion at Riverside Park in Beloit in 2013.[16]

Organizers planned activities that would allow family members to know more about each other. A baby pictures contest at the reunion in Park City, Utah, in 1992 recognized not the most beautiful baby but the ability to identify the most babies.[17] Thirty-eight photos of babies were entered in the contest, a feat in itself for it required the older generation to acquire and post photos by email to Harry. One year there was a contest for prognostications: Who would be the next Wong cousin to marry, and which couple would have the next child? There were also votes for "chip off the old block"—the child who most resembled their mother or father—most doting grandparent, and most active child. Winners in these categories were Rick Wong as chip off the block of his father, George; Mary Wong Palmer as most doting grandparent; and David's son, Alex Wong (age four in 1997), as the most active child.

The reunion has become the central means of passing along family wisdom and traditions and for making connections with family members. Stories are told and retold, new members are lovingly welcomed into the family fold, and Wong values—first among them, loyalty to family—are passed along. Seventy-six Wong family members attended the most recent reunion, hosted by Harry and Jean Wong and their children in Salt Lake City in 2018.[18] Attendees interacted and reminisced with the help of photo albums of previous reunions. During this family reunion, the celebration of family history included interviews with a historian who was attempting to pull the stories together into a coherent narrative of Charles's and Yee Shee's immigration and their children's upbringing.

Return to Mong Dee Village

Mary Wong Palmer

As she was putting the Wong family history together, Mary Wong Palmer decided she needed to try to find her father's birthplace. As the last stop on a highlights tour in China in 2008, she took a group of family—including her husband and children, David, Jim, and Shari Palmer—and friends to Guangdong province to search for Mong Dee village. In planning the trip, Mary reached out to relatives who had lived in the village earlier in their lives. Cousin Terry Lee helped by writing the village name in Chinese characters and providing a verbal map to the area. Cousin Susan Toy sent a recent map of the area that included the names of other nearby townships, notably Duanfen, outside of Taishan City.[1]

The group left Hong Kong in late October. They took a ferry to Guangzhou and then a bus to Taishan City, where they stayed in a hotel that had been constructed for overseas Chinese who were traveling to the area, as the Palmers were, to visit their ancestral villages. This population was large, for so many men had emigrated from the area that more than twice the population of the Taishan area now lived overseas. They found guides in each area they visited in China, including in Guangdong. When they arrived in Taishan, a national guide did some further research for them and accompanied them on their voyage.

From Taishan to the village the group traveled through a rural and quiet countryside. They left Taishan City headed for the township of Duanfen in a minivan early in the day, before the weather became hot and humid. The road they followed was modern with many lanes, but it had fewer cars than they had seen in other parts of China. On either side of the road they saw lush, almost tropical countryside with fish farms and many small, neatly planted fields of vegetables, sugar cane, pineapples, bananas, oranges, and rice that was being harvested. It was also a countryside in transition; they saw new factories, roads, and bridges under construction. They found villages that were not on their map and in each location they looked for the oldest person to ask whether he or she knew anything about the village of Mong Dee.

In Duanfen Township they were directed to a taxi stand where men and motorbikes gathered. One man in the group said he knew the way to Mong Dee, so the van followed him into an older section of the township and down a road that had older, grayish stone buildings with balconies and carved tops, clear evidence from the early twentieth-century boom associated with overseas wealth. They passed a market and Mary wondered whether this was the same market her family had shopped in a century earlier. Soon the road became too narrow and unpaved for their minivan, so the visitors got out and started to walk. They were not sure how far it would be, but their journey improved when the road narrowed to become "a path surrounded by pretty flowers, butterflies, ponds, and gardens." They carried umbrellas to shield from the muggy heat of the sun. After about forty-five minutes, they saw a tall gate with Chinese characters across the top and down both sides. Their guide excitedly told Mary that this was the Wong Village of Mong Dee, or Wang Dee in Mandarin, and said that the Chinese characters on the gate matched the written characters that Terry Lee had written for Mary.

Modern Mong Dee was quite unassuming. From where they stood among the houses, the group could see rice paddies and guava trees in addition to men with water buffaloes tilling the fields. A stark impression of the village was delivered by Mary's son, Jim Palmer, who is a physician in the United States. Jim saw what his ancestors had fled. "Over one hundred years later, [the village] hadn't progressed in any significant way." Jim saw wrecked houses everywhere, "pure shacks," and he noted that the houses that were hundreds of years old looked better than the ones built in the early twentieth century because of the large bricks used in their construction. There was no school or market. Jim noted there were communal bathrooms, one for men

Mong Dee village
gate, 2008.
(David Palmer)

and one for women, and there appeared to be no running water or electricity, though the houses did have gas.[2]

For her part, Mary was charmed by the village and its setting.[3] Big hills or small mountains surrounded the area. The whole village was only 125 yards by 60 yards, with gates at both ends erected by the earlier expatriates. Long, parallel buildings separated by narrow alleys perched on a slightly elevated slope so that rainwater would run down. The alleyways were clean and improvements to properties were evident, such as a new security door on one house. There were, however, elaborate decorations on the buildings, evidence of wealth from early in the twentieth century, that had not been maintained. And right in the center of the village was a large open area shaded by two huge banyan trees that overlooked a large fishpond. This was the fishpond that so many of her relatives had described, both in their immigration interviews and to her.

Mary guessed that only about one hundred people still lived in the village, considerably fewer than the four hundred her cousin Albert Wong had described. Still, she thought the housing could easily accommodate that larger number. They saw mainly children and older people and were told that the children attend school in another town.

What they did not find were relatives: not a single Wong remained in Mong Dee, and no one they spoke to remembered any Wong from the past. They had not expected to find anyone closely related, since reports from the village were dated. Their most recent report was from a cousin that Mary and David met on their trip to Guangzhou in 1984, already twenty-four years earlier.[4] And Yee Shee, who had already died when the group went in 1984,

Farmer between banyan trees with fishpond in background, Mong Dee, 2008. (David Palmer)

had left Mong Dee sixty years earlier than that, in 1923. Yee Shee's last interaction with anyone from Mong Dee had been in 1972, when she reunited with a woman who had been her best friend there and who had recently arrived in the United States.

People did seem to know where Shitou, Yee Shee's village, was. To Mary's familial knowledge, Shitou was a half day's walk away. When asked, people pointed to some distant buildings, saying it was part of that village, but they said that the main part of Shitou was beyond the next hill, too far to walk. Finally, they saw, but did not get the chance to explore, a cemetery on the nearby hillside, where they knew Wong Doo Set and many of his brothers were buried. After Mary returned to the United States, her cousin Gloria Wong Moy gave her a detailed map of the New Village which, according to the immigration records, is near the cemetery.[5] Mary did feel a real connection to her ancestors and especially to her father, who had left Mong Dee one hundred years earlier.

Mary Wong Palmer consulting with the oldest person living in Mong Dee, 2008. (David Palmer)

Mary Wong Palmer knew that many villagers had been relocated during the Cultural Revolution, but she was still surprised to find that no one in Mong Dee knew the Wongs. War, famine, and political relocation help explain the population change in the village. During the decades of vast emigration, populations of *huaqiao* villages, such as Mong Dee, consisted mainly of elderly returnees and women and children dependents of men working abroad. But war and famine during the Japanese occupation, the Chinese Civil War, and World War II decimated village populations. One-quarter of the population of Taishan county died in a famine that began in 1943.[6] More villagers left after the war, when the United States and Canada made their policies more accommodating to allow families to reunite abroad. Additionally, many *huaqiao* left for Hong Kong in the 1950s, when Chinese policies seemed very severe, and then again in the Red Guard era, when people with overseas ties suffered persecution and had their homes looted. Finally, as historian Madeline Hsu writes, thousands of Chinese emigrated during the 1980s and 1990s. Between 1978 and 1986, an average of 8,118 people left Taishan each year, and 16.2 percent of the county's population emigrated in 1980 alone, nearly 75 percent of them to the United States.[7] Still, the Palmers had been hopeful that someone would remember Mary's relatives.

As the Palmer group left Mong Dee, they were unsure they had even found the correct village. Although Mary looked closely at people in the village and saw some who looked Han Chinese, like the Wongs, many looked very different and were possibly members of ethnic minorities. More tellingly, no one in the village spoke the same dialect of Chinese that Mary had learned from her mother. That she knew Chinese at all had been established on the earlier trip to Guangzhou. Mary's children reported that they used to tease their mother about not really speaking Chinese because they had never heard Mary communicate successfully with other Chinese people in the United States. On the trip to China in 1984, however, Mary met up with a great-aunt from Mong Dee and spoke to her very fluently.[8] Still, finding no one who spoke the same dialect in Mong Dee in 2008 suggests that displacement *had* occurred, for presumably if they were not in the ancestral village, they were very close to it.

In the end, Mary believes it *was* the right place. First, when her cousin Susan Toy saw the photos of the village, particularly images of the banyan trees and the fishpond, she confirmed that it was definitely Mong Dee. Susan had lived in the village for three years during World War II, from the time she was thirteen to sixteen years old. Susan also informed Mary that all of the photos depicted the old section of town, so they had not visited the section of town that Mary's grandfather had called the New Village at his immigration interview in 1925. Second, in response to a query by Mary's sister-in-law, Cynthia Wong Stamberger, the Taishan Overseas Chinese Affairs office confirmed that the photos she sent in were of the village that had been called Mong Dee in the past.[9]

In Mong Dee, Mary connected to her history and ancestors, though many questions remained. She wondered how Charles and Yee Shee felt as they left this place for the uncertain life in America. Did they think they would ever return? How did they get to Duanfen and then to Macao or Hong Kong to get the ocean liner to Seattle? What did they carry with them? Were they detained and interrogated? Still, Mary had an overwhelming feeling of gratitude to her parents and an obligation to carry forward their legacies. Mary ended her narrative about the return to Mong Dee:

> I have told my family that we all should feel grateful for the sacrifices our parents made for us, that we might have a better future. I feel at peace, now that my lifelong dream to see where my parents came from was realized.

Appendix

Shari Palmer and Andy Dimock wrote this play for their younger relatives to perform at the 2005 Wong family reunion in San Diego, California.

Prelude

NARRATOR 1: Alex Dereix
NARRATOR 2: Alex Wong
MICHELE: Michele Ring
CAILI: Caili West
CALLIE: Callie Wong

Michele, Callie, and Caili are sitting together looking at a photograph album. The photographs are projected on the wall behind them.

MICHELE: So many cousins, and aunts and uncles, and great-aunts and great-uncles!

CAILI: Tell me about it.

MICHELE: And I keep hearing different stories about how our family got to America.

CAILI: And how are we related to you again? Some kind of cousin?

MICHELE: My dad told me we were third cousins. Or was it second cousins once-removed?

CALLIE: But who are all these people? *(pointing to the pictures)*

CAILI: And who are all these people? *(pointing at the audience)*

NARRATOR 1: These are some of the founding fathers and mothers of the Wong clan in America. *(pointing to the pictures on the screen)*

NARRATOR 2: And these are the descendants and relatives of the founders. *(pointing at the audience)*

NARRATOR 1: The real story of how our family got to the United States is part of the larger story of the Chinese in America, and in some ways is typical of that tale.

NARRATOR 2: But in other ways it is quite unusual.

NARRATOR 1: It's a story that includes tragedy and heartbreak.

NARRATOR 2: And one that includes courage and happiness.

NARRATOR 1: Let's watch as Yee Shee and Wong Theong leave China for the United States.

(Michele, Callie, and Caili leave stage.)

Scene 1. On the USS *President McKinley* en route from Hong Kong to Seattle, 1923

NARRATOR 1: Alex Dereix

NARRATOR 2: Lauren Wong

CHARLES WONG: Alex West

YEE SHEE (pregnant): Caili West

JOHN PEARSON (railway engineer): Steven Ring

REV. ARTHUR SLOAN (missionary): Alex Wong

MRS. ARTHUR SLOAN (missionary): Michelle Ring

CHINESE WAITER: William Palmer

Yee Shee and Charles stand waving from the ship's deck. The rest of the company wave back at them from a distance, calling farewells. Fade.

NARRATOR 2: In 1923, Yee Shee and Wong Theong had been married for ten years, but had lived together for less than two years.

NARRATOR 1: The rest of the time, Wong Theong—known as Charles Wong—worked in the United States with his uncles and cousins while Yee Shee lived with his family in the village.

NARRATOR 2: This was a common arrangement for the Gold Mountain sojourners, as the men called themselves

NARRATOR 1: China at this time was beset by political upheavals, banditry, and poverty.

NARRATOR 2: The United States was no paradise either. After initially being welcomed into the country as laborers, the Chinese were now confronted with highly discriminatory laws and immigration controls.

NARRATOR 1: Nonetheless, Charles Wong saw opportunity in America, and he wanted his wife with him.

NARRATOR 2: Here we see them saying farewell to friends and family at the dock as they embark for Seattle. They will never see most of these people again.

(Sitting in chairs at a table, eating.)

YEE SHEE: Tell me again about where we're going.

CHARLES: Beloit, Wisconsin. It's not far from Chicago.

YEE SHEE: Are there other Chinese in Beloit?

CHARLES: You mean apart from those of us who work in the restaurant? No. *(long pause)* But it's a nice little town. There were already plenty of Chinese restaurants in Chicago. We thought we'd try someplace new. And the Chop House has been very successful!

YEE SHEE: And where are we going to live?

CHARLES: Well, we'll stay behind the restaurant for a few days until I can find us an apartment. I hope to buy a house soon!

YEE SHEE: *(patting her stomach)* We'll need a home to bring our baby to once he is born.

(A man comes in and joins them at the table.)

PEARSON: Hello. I'm John Pearson.

CHARLES: I'm Charles Wong, and this is my wife, Yee Shee.

(They sit and eat in silence for a moment.)

CHARLES: Your Chinese is excellent.

PEARSON: Thank you. I've been doing business in Shanghai, and I find it useful. Is Seattle your final destination?

CHARLES: No, we're going on to Wisconsin.

PEARSON: *(with disbelief)* Wisconsin! Don't see many Chinese there, I guess. I would have thought you were in business in San Francisco or Chicago. I do business with some Chinese folks there. I'm with the railroads.

CHARLES: Ah, yes. I did work in Utah for a time. I am in the restaurant business.

PEARSON: Hmm. We aren't building too many more rail lines. Those Chinese fellers sure did work hard, though. Better than any other crew I ever saw.

(A man and a woman join their table.)

PEARSON: Hello, Reverend, Mrs. Sloan. I was just saying that I used to work with Celestials on the railroad and that they were fine workers.

REV. SLOAN: Yes, we have found the Chinese to be very hardworking and clever. If we can but bring them to accept the true Christian church . . . *(he sighs)* *(to Charles)* Hello, permit me to introduce myself and my wife, Arthur and Elizabeth Sloan.

CHARLES: Pleased to meet you. Charles Wong and my wife, Yee Shee.

MRS. SLOAN: *(to Yee Shee)* You are from Hong Kong?

YEE SHEE: We come from Toisan, near Canton.

MRS. SLOAN: Oh yes, I know the area. My husband and I have been working near Canton for the past two years. I hear there are terrible problems with bandits in the outlying villages.

YEE SHEE: In our village a few years ago, the warlords kidnapped all of the schoolchildren and demanded a ransom! Charles and other men in America had to send the money home so we could pay it. That kind of crime is one reason for our journey.

MRS. SLOAN: Well, and the terrible poverty! I know you must not be peasants since you're traveling first class, but I tell you we don't see so many poor people in Wisconsin!

CHARLES: Indeed. We're going to Beloit, Wisconsin, where I operate a restaurant.

REV. SLOAN: Well, isn't that a coincidence! Perhaps you can come to our church in Sheboygan.

CHARLES: We'll certainly do that if we're ever in the area.

(Pearson and the Sloans excuse themselves and leave the table. A waiter approaches the table.)

WAITER: Pardon me. Is it true that you have citizenship papers?

CHARLES: Yes. Why do you ask?

WAITER: Well, I was wondering if you knew anyone who had a son about my age. You know, so I could get to the Gold Mountain, too. I have some money.

CHARLES: No, I'm sorry. I don't know anyone. Better for you to do your filial duty at home, however.

WAITER: Easy for you to say. I can't get decent work at home, and I get seasick on this boat. *(he groans)*

CHARLES: I know things aren't so good in China right now. But you know it's hard to be Chinese in America as well.

WAITER: Oh, I know! The Chinese men down in steerage are all working to memorize their stories for immigration. And I hear Chinese have no rights at all in some places. Still, aren't you proof of the opportunities in America?

CHARLES: My family has done quite well, yes. We were always enterprising though.

WAITER: *(he addresses Yee Shee)* With the exclusion laws, I haven't seen a Chinese woman on this boat in years.

YEE SHEE: Yes, I got that impression from everyone staring at me. But surely there are more Chinese women once we get to America.

WAITER: No—you should see the Chinatowns. Hardly a respectable Chinese woman anywhere. Most men find it too hard to get in themselves, let alone bring a wife. *(he pauses and looks at her hard)* You're a brave woman.

YEE SHEE: I'd rather be with my husband than back in Toisan living with my in-laws. At least this way my child will grow up knowing his father.

CHARLES: If you ever get to Chicago, ask for Wong Doo Set. He's my father, and he can help you find a position in a restaurant! We can always use a good waiter.

Scene 2. 1015 Lincoln Avenue, Beloit, 1938

NARRATOR 1: Alex Dereix

NARRATOR 2: Lauren Wong

YEE SHEE WONG: Caili West

GIM WONG (14): Alex West

FUNG WONG (12): Mara Hyatt

GEORGE WONG (11): Steven Ring

HELEN WONG (8): Rebecca Fortsch

HARRY WONG (6): Andrew Wong

FRANK WONG (3): Laurence Palmer

MARY WONG (2): Helen Lude

MRS. ANTONSEN (neighbor): Michele Ring

NING (BILL) WONG: Alex Wong

Yee Shee and Charles stand with all seven children in a happy family tableau.

NARRATOR 1: The Wong family soon grew to include Gim *(Gim steps forward and waves)*, born in 1924, Fung *(Fung waves)* in 1926, George *(George waves)* in 1928, Helen *(Helen waves)* in 1931, Harry *(Harry waves)* in 1933, Frank *(Frank waves)* in 1935, and finally, Mary *(Mary waves)* in 1937.

(On a slide in background we see each of the children in photos as they are named.)

NARRATOR 2: The Chop House was one of the most popular restaurants in Beloit.

NARRATOR 1: Charles Wong was an enthusiastic but notoriously bad driver, who enjoyed taking all the kids for car rides around the block in the afternoon.

(Kids all pile in "car" with Charles for ride.)

NARRATOR 2: But in July 1938, tragedy.

NARRATOR 1: Charles Wong was shot and killed by a cousin over an argument in the restaurant.

NARRATOR 2: Yee Shee was left alone to raise seven children, from the ages of one to fourteen years, in a foreign land.

(The music changes to a sad note. Charles puts on a hat, turns, and leaves the stage. Yee Shee and her late husband's half-brother sit talking)

YEE SHEE: *(holding a folded sheet of paper)* This is a very kind offer.

BILL: We all feel terrible about what happened to Charles.

YEE SHEE: It has been very hard since his death, but this is a difficult decision. The children are all little Americans now. They speak much better English than Chinese. They go to church and American school.

BILL: But who will help you support seven children without a husband?

YEE SHEE: Gim and Fung are old enough to work. And even the younger children help out how they can. Our neighbors have been very kind, too.

BILL: Still, neighbors aren't the same as family!

YEE SHEE: Yes, of course, but I need to think about this. *(she pauses)* Gim, come here!

GIM: *(coming in)* What is it, mother?

YEE SHEE: Your father's half-brother, Uncle Bill, brings a letter from Hong Kong, from Uncle Doo Sung.

GIM: What does he say?

YEE SHEE: He is offering to arrange for our family to go to Hong Kong, where he would help support us.

(Fung comes in, holding little Mary.)

FUNG: What is it?

GIM: Father's uncle wants us to go live in Hong Kong where they can help us.

FUNG: *(subdued)* Oh. Are we going to?

YEE SHEE: That's what I wanted to talk to you about.

GIM: Aren't we doing enough to help here? I know I could help more in the restaurant. I could finish school later.

FUNG: And I could take in more sewing! I don't think I want to live in China. Don't they bind women's feet there?

YEE SHEE: You two are already doing so much. Your cousins have offered to buy our share of the restaurant, and I've decided to accept. That money will help us live without you sacrificing your education. Besides, it's for you and the younger children that I'm thinking about Hong Kong. Wouldn't it be better to be closer to family, among other Chinese people?

BILL: My uncle and his wife would very much like to help.

GIM: But we don't know Hong Kong! All we know is Beloit! And we are always hearing from relatives about all the troubles in China.

(George comes in carrying a radio. He sits down and fiddles with it. Harry comes out tossing a ball.)

FUNG: Look at those boys. They're little Americans! Maybe future engineers.

(George yelps and shakes his hand. Harry grabs it to look at it.)

FUNG: Or maybe doctors!

(Frank walks by reading a picture book. He sits near the other boys but continues reading.)

YEE SHEE: True. And look at little Frank, too. There are no more imperial examinations in China, but he's a born scholar.

(Helen comes in and hugs her mother.)

HELEN: Mom—can I help make dinner?

YEE SHEE: Not right now, Helen, but you can weed the garden. Please take Mary with you.

(Helen sighs, but takes baby Mary from Fung and goes into the yard to tend the garden, tugging Mary by the hand.)

BILL: They are wonderful children!

YEE SHEE: *(modestly)* They are not so special. Harry got a B on his report card last week. And George is having trouble with his asthma again. I'm afraid we spoil Mary. Poor thing. She'll never know her father.

(Mrs. Antonsen comes to the door bearing a bag and a plate of cookies.)

MRS. ANTONSEN: Hello. May I come in?

YEE SHEE: You know you are always welcome! Please meet my husband's brother, Bill. Bill, Mrs. Antonsen, my neighbor.

MRS. ANTONSEN: *(to Bill)* Pleased to meet you. *(to Yee Shee, handing the bag and plate to Fung)* I brought you some anise seed cookies and some German potato salad; I made too much!

FUNG: Oh, I love anise cookies!

YEE SHEE: You are too kind! Thank you.

MRS. ANTONSEN: Well, you are very generous with fruit from your garden and your holiday chop suey! Oh, and I almost forgot. I hope George can come by and mow our yard on Saturday? I can easier spare the quarter than the time these days!

GIM: If he can't do it, I will, Mrs. Antonsen.

MRS. ANTONSEN: Thank you, Gim. You're a credit to your mother, as are you, Fung.

YEE SHEE: Don't spoil them! They are good children, true, but you are a good neighbor.

MRS. ANTONSEN: I have to run. I'll see you soon. Goodbye! *(exiting)*

BILL: You do have good neighbors.

YEE SHEE: Yes, this feels almost like a village. The butcher saves me the chicken feet and the giblets. The fishmonger saves the fish head and bones. *(aside)* Amazing what these Americans let go to waste!

(They sit and watch the children for a moment.)

YEE SHEE: I've decided. We're going to stay here.

BILL: Are you quite sure?

YEE SHEE: Yes, I'm sure. I don't think things will be any easier in Hong Kong. Your uncle already has his own family to care for, and my children are at home here.

BILL: What about your property in Hong Kong?

YEE SHEE: I'll keep it in case we eventually decide to go back. Who knows, maybe this won't always be the right place for us. But for now, we'll stay.

Scene 3. First Wong reunion, Beloit, 1969

NARRATOR 1: Alex Dereix

NARRATOR 2: Lauren Wong

YEE SHEE: Caili West

GIM: Alex West

FUNG: Mara Hyatt

GEORGE: Alex Wong

HELEN: Rebecca Fortsch

HARRY: Andrew Wong

FRANK: Steven Ring

MARY: Natasha Wong

Yee Shee sits surrounded by her grandchildren, holding the youngest baby on her lap (James Galloway).

NARRATOR 1: By 1969, Yee Shee's seven children have all graduated from college and, all but Frank, married with children. Gim *(Gim waves)* is married to Marion and has had four children; Fung *(Fung waves)* and her husband Al have three children; George *(George waves)* is married to Joyce and has had six children; Helen *(Helen waves)* and Jim have three children; Harry *(Harry waves)* is married to Jean and has four children; Frank is recently married to Cynthia *(Frank waves)* but has no children yet; and Mary *(Mary waves)* and David have two children.

NARRATOR 2: Yee Shee now has twenty grandchildren. Eventually, by 2005, her descendants will include twenty-two grandchildren and thirty-three great-grandchildren.

NARRATOR 1: Since 1939, she has travelled twice to Hong Kong as well as all over the United States.

NARRATOR 2: And she naturalized—took U.S. citizenship—in 1959.

NARRATOR 1: Here the family reflects on its past at the first ever Wong reunion.

FUNG: *(looking at her mother)* Isn't it wonderful for all of us to be together, George!

GEORGE: Yes, it's hard now that not everyone is in the same city. Of course, you still live in Beloit, Fung.

FUNG: Yes, like mom says, I'm just a small-town girl.

GIM: Hey, I'm still in Beloit, too. Guess that makes me a small-town boy.

(Yee Shee comes over.)

FUNG: Mom—do you remember when you thought about taking us all back to Hong Kong?

YEE SHEE: Of course! I think of it often.

GIM: Do you ever regret your decision?

YEE SHEE: Not for a moment. When you took me to Hong Kong in 1948, I saw how dirty and crowded it was. Too big city. Too rude. I prefer Beloit.

FRANK: Do you ever miss China?

YEE SHEE: No. I saw when I went back that everyone I cared about in the village was already gone. And oh, those Communists! *(shaking her fist)* They're bad people. Even the old ladies they make work so

hard! Much, much better here. I have my own house. All my kids and
grandkids so successful, even if some of them do live too far away.

HELEN: It is pretty impressive that we all graduated from college.

HARRY: Not to mention the graduate degrees.

MARY: You did okay, doctor.

GEORGE: We've turned out to be pretty complete Americans. Gim and I
both served in the military.

YEE SHEE: I didn't like that part so much.

FRANK: But that's a sign of truly belonging to a place. When you came,
most Chinese couldn't even get citizenship!

YEE SHEE: I'm an American citizen! I decided to do it after my trip back
to China.

GIM: That's right, you told the immigration officer that one of the
founding fathers was Georgie Washington!

YEE SHEE: Wasn't that right?

FUNG: That's exactly right! Why shouldn't he be Georgie?

NARRATOR 1: As the children of Yee Shee and Charles Wong talk, their
children prepare a surprise.

NARRATOR 2: This then, is the origin of two most venerated Wong
reunion traditions: first, the traditional family skit, which began with
the Traveling Bubblegum.

(*Everyone old enough to chew gum stands in a line blowing bubbles. One steps out
of line, pretending to discard her gum on the floor. An unsuspecting passerby steps
on the imaginary gum and looks at his shoe with dismay.*)

NARRATOR 1: And the second thirty-five-year-old tradition . . .

NARRATOR 2: The Big Box . . .

(*Members of the first- and second-generation descendants introduce the Big Box
theme for this reunion.*)

Notes

Introduction

1. See Beatrice McKenzie, "To Know a Citizen: Birthright Citizenship Documents Regimes in U.S. History," in *Citizenship in Question*, ed. Jacqueline Stevens and Benjamin Lawrance (Durham, NC: Duke University Press, 2017).

2. The 1981 interview transcript of Helen Wong Way's interview of Ben Wong allowed me to unravel the identity of the Wong grandfather, Wong Ben Yuk (a.k.a. Wong Doo Set). See transcript in the Wong Family Papers, Beloit College Archives, Beloit, Wisconsin (hereafter WFP). Survey results in WFP.

3. Erika Lee, *At America's Gates: Chinese Immigration during the Exclusion Era, 1882–1943* (Chapel Hill: University of North Carolina Press, 2003); Mae Ngai, *Impossible Subjects: Illegal Aliens and the Making of Modern America* (Princeton, NJ: Princeton University Press, 2005). Books published after 2010 were also of critical importance to this research, especially Huping Ling, *Chinese Chicago: Race, Transnational Migration, and Community since 1870* (Stanford, CA: Stanford University Press, 2012), and Him Mark Lai, *Him Mark Lai: Autobiography of a Chinese American Historian*, ed. Judy Yung et al. (Los Angeles: Asian American Studies Center and Chinese Historical Society of America 2011).

4. Exceptions include Huping Ling, *Chinese Chicago*, and Adam McKeown, *Chinese Migrant Networks and Cultural Change: Peru, Chicago, Hawaii, 1900–1936* (Chicago: University of Chicago Press, 2001).

5. I presented research on Beloit's globalization, on Yee Shee, and on Wong Doo Set (Mary's grandfather) at three professional conferences where I benefited from the critical input and enthusiasm of other academics. "Beloit Wisconsin 1896–1914: Global Integration of a Midwestern Industrial Town," in *The Annual Proceedings of the Wealth and Well-Being of Nations, 2018–2019*, vol. 11, ed. Diep Phan (Beloit, WI: Beloit College Press, 2019). "At the Intersection of Race, Gender, Sexuality, and Social Class: An Examination of a Chinese Woman's Immigration in Early Twentieth Century United States," Women's History Conference, Fez, Morocco, June 2019.

"Chinese-American Birthright Citizenship Claims, 1888–1931," American Political Science Association, September 2019.

6. The bulk of Mary Wong Palmer's materials have now been donated to the Beloit College Archives. See WFP.

7. Oral history interviews of Fung Wong Scholz, Harry Wong, and Mary Wong Palmer.

8. Fung Wong Scholz, Harry Wong, and Mary Wong Palmer suggested which of their nieces and nephews I should interview, focusing on those who knew best their mother, Yee Shee Gok. I interviewed at least two of each sibling's children so I would have comparable material for them. In all, I interviewed twenty-six Wong family members. From the second generation, Mary (June 2010), Fung (April 13, 2018), Harry (June 2, 2018), and Cynthia Tsao Wong Stamberger (July 14, 2018). From the third generation, Lisa Wong Fortsch (June 18, 2018), David Wong (June 18, 2018), Jeff Wong (July 14, 2018), Stacey Wong West (July 14, 2018), Mary Scholz Hoffert (July 15, 2018), Chris Wong (July 14, 2018), Wendy Wong Dereix (July 14, 2018), Lani Way (July 14, 2018), Tim Wong (July 14, 2018), Cathy Wong Ring (July 14, 2018), Jim Palmer (July 15, 2018), Jon Way (July 15, 2018), Shari Palmer (July 15, 2018), and Lori Way Galloway (July 15, 2018). I also interviewed Ronald Lee (July 14, 2018), Catherine Lee (July 14, 2018), and Theresa Lee Yih and Bob Yih (October 24, 2019). Later I interviewed Cherie Scholz Baker with her mother and sister (February 26, 2019), John Wong (April 16, 2019), and Alan Scholz (May 15, 2019). I also interviewed one member of the fourth generation, Alexandra (Alex) Dereix, granddaughter of Gim Wong and daughter of Wendy Dereix (July 29, 2020). At Mary Wong Palmer's request, I interviewed my colleague Ian Nie (June 5, 2020), emeritus professor of music at Beloit College.

9. This book uses "half brother" to denote that two children had the same father but different mothers but "step-uncle" to denote the relationship between uncle and niece/nephew; family members always referred to their father's half brothers as step-uncles.

10. When asked directly in an interview, Harry indicated that his future brother-in-law, Al Scholz, helped Harry get hired in the foundry because it met Harry's primary objective, the possibility of earning time and a half pay. Harry Wong interview, June 2, 2018.

11. Ian Haney Lopez, *White by Law: The Legal Construction of Race* (New York: New York University Press, 1996; 2006); George Sanchez, "Race, Nation, and Culture in Recent Immigration Studies," *Journal of American Ethnic History* 18, no. 4 (Summer 1999); Lee, *At America's Gates*; Ngai, *Impossible Subjects*; Anna Pegler-Gordon, "Debating the Racial Turn in U.S. Ethnic and Immigration History," *Journal of American Ethnic History* (Winter 2017): 40–53.

12. Judy Yung, "In Our Own Words: Reclaiming Chinese American Women's History," in *Ethnic Historians and the Mainstream: Shaping America's Immigration*

Story, ed. Alan Kraut and David Gerber (New Brunswick, NJ: Rutgers University Press, 2013), 111–27, 121; Mireya Loza, "Ephemeral to Enduring: The Politics of Recording and Exhibiting Bracero Memory," *The Public Historian* 38, no. 2 (May 2016): 23–41, 30–31. See also Oral History Association, "Oral History Association Code of Ethics," at https://www.oralhistory.org/oha-statement-on-ethics/.

13. Loza, "Ephemeral to Enduring," 32.

14. Alessandro Portelli, "What Makes Oral History Different?" in *The Oral History Reader*, ed. Robert Perks and Alistair Thomson (New York: Taylor & Francis Group, 2015), 32–42, 41.

15. WFP. This has been a richly rewarding undertaking. It is rare to be given close access to a family's complex dynamics, and I very much appreciate the opportunity. Although I have relied extensively on critiques of the manuscript by Wong family members, colleagues, and the academic readers selected by the University of Wisconsin Press, any errors that remain are my own.

16. Rich secondary sources for this study include Ling, *Chinese Chicago*; Lee, *At America's Gates*; Him Mark Lai, *Him Mark Lai*; and McKeown, *Chinese Migrant Networks*.

Chapter 1. Transnational Migration in the Exclusion Era

1. Fung Wong Scholz interview, April 3, 2018. Grandfather Wong had asthma and needed an escape from Chicago summers.

2. "Wong Family Reminiscences," February 23, 1991, WFP.

3. This birthdate is an estimate based on the photo from 1912 and family interviews. Families typically had a child born every two years, and there could have been a sister in between him and his younger brother, believed to have been born in 1874. "Letter from Immigrant Inspector Jos H. Scully to Inspector in Charge, Chinese Division, Immigration Station, Angel Island, Cal., 9/26/12," in 30734/3–23 WONG Ben Yuk file, National Archives Record Administration, San Bruno (hereafter NARA San Bruno).

4. This concept exists in other parts of the world. Examples include the southern Italian town of Torregreca, whose men were guest workers in Germany, and the West Indian island of Montserrat, which sent emigrants to Britain in the 1950s and 1960s. Lynn Pan, ed., *Encyclopedia of the Chinese Overseas* (Cambridge, MA: Harvard University Press, 1999), 27.

5. Him Mark Lai, *Him Mark Lai*, 9–12. Also see June Mei, "Socioeconomic Origins of Emigration from Guangdong to California, 1850–1882," *Modern China* 5, no. 4 (October 1979): 463–501: "Families with land that was not worth the cost of passage would also pool resources with relatives to send one member of the clan abroad" (482).

6. Bob Wong said that his uncle Wong Ben Yuk and his three sons died in a flu epidemic. After Bob's father Wong Doo Set took his brother's place, he also

sponsored three nephews, his third brother's sons, as immigrants to the United States. Interview of Bob Wong by Helen Wong Way and George Wong, June 15, 1982, WFP.

7. This material was explored in a recent paper delivered by the author at the American Political Science Association meeting in Washington, DC, on August 31, 2019, "Chinese-American Birthright Citizenship Claims, 1888–1931." See also McKenzie, "To Know a Citizen."

8. Chinese calculate ages differently. When a child is born, he or she is a year old. This book offers ages in the manner calculated in the United States.

9. Ethan Blue, "Finding Margins on Borders: Shipping Firms and Immigration Control Across Settler Space," *Occasion: Interdisciplinary Studies in the Humanities* 5 (March 1, 2013): 1–20, https://arcade.stanford.edu/sites/default/files/article_pdfs/OCCASION_v05i01_Blue_032213_0.pdf.

10. *Daily Alta California*, May 22, 1887, January 14, 1888, March 14, 1888, April 13, 1888.

11. We know nothing definitive about Wong Sang, although a man named Wong Sang conducted business at 103 Dupont, in San Francisco, in 1899. *San Francisco Call*, February 26, 1899.

12. "Because He Could Not Land," *Daily Alta California*, September 21, 1888.

13. "In the District Court of the United States, Northern District of California. In the Matter of Wong Ben Yuk, On Habeas Corpus, 9/14/88," in 30734/3–23 WONG Ben Yuk file, NARA San Bruno.

14. NARA documents. In 30734/3–23 WONG Ben Yuk file, NARA San Bruno.

15. Interview of Wong Ben Yuk, aboard SS *Korea*, March 27, 1903. He said he'd been born in the United States in 1874, entered the United States as a citizen after a habeas corpus case on March 27, 1889. He entered again on November 29, 1896, returned to China and returned via the SS *Korea* on March 26, 1903. He was admitted that time on April 6, 1903, having spent two weeks in custody on the ship. In 30734/3–23 WONG Ben Yuk file, NARA San Bruno.

16. Bob Wong was certain his father's parents (Doo Set's and Ben Yuk's parents) had never been to the United States. Bob had been born in Mong Dee village in 1922 and immigrated to the United States in 1931. Interview of Bob Wong by Helen Wong Way and George Wong, June 15, 1982, WFP.

17. Pan, *Encyclopedia of the Chinese Overseas*, 35.

18. The Pan volume suggests that the person left at home would farm, but the Wongs have no knowledge of relatives farming in Mong Dee. Mary Wong Palmer believes they leased their land to farmers who lived in the area. Mary said relatives informed her that Wong Doo Set's third brother, Wong Doo Yee, who was very smart and considered adept at financial affairs, was selected to remain in the village and manage overseas remittances as well as the family who remained in China. Mary Wong Palmer interview, March 2, 2021.

19. Pan, *Encyclopedia of the Chinese Overseas*, 35.

20. Wong Doo Set's granddaughter-in-law, Cynthia Wong Stamberger, stated in her interview that Doo Set established a medical practice in a pharmacy at 766 Clay Street, in San Francisco's Chinatown. Indeed, Doo Set offered that address at immigration interviews twice, once in 1925, when he said he lived there, and once in 1929, when he said a document could be sent to that address. Because the Beloit Wongs and Doo Set's son, Ben, only ever mention Chicago as Doo Set's residence, whether he also worked in San Francisco remains a question. Cynthia Wong Stamberger interview, July 14, 2018, WFP. See NARA documents in additional evidence interview for Mun Bin and Mun Nging in 1925, and certificate of identity application for Wong Mun Bin, 1929, WFP.

21. Pan, *Encyclopedia of the Chinese Overseas*, 36. Erika Lee indicates that between 1801 and 1900 an estimated 2.5 million Chinese migrated to Southeast Asia, the United States, the Pacific Islands of Hawaii, Tahiti, and Western Samoa, and to Canada, Australia, New Zealand, the West Indies, South America, and Africa. Erika Lee, *The Making of Asian America: A History* (New York: Simon & Shuster, 2015), 47.

22. Pan, *Encyclopedia of the Chinese Overseas*, 56.

23. See chapters 1–3 in Lee, *Making of Asian America*.

24. Mei, "Socioeconomic Origins of Emigration," 486.

25. Lee, *Making of Asian America*, 72. See also Gordon Chang, *Ghosts of Gold Mountain: The Epic Story of Chinese Who Built the Transcontinental Railroad* (Stanford, CA: Stanford University Press, 2019).

26. Lee, *Making of Asian America*, 59. See also Ling, *Chinese Chicago*.

27. Yoneyuki Sugita, "The Rise of an American Principle in China: A Reinterpretation of the First Open Door Notes toward China," in *Trans-Pacific Relations: America, Europe, and Asia in the Twentieth Century*, ed. Richard J. Jensen, Jon Thares Davidann, and Yoneyuki Sugita (Westport, CT: Greenwood, 2003), 3–20. See also Thomas G. Otte, *The China Question: Great Power Rivalry and British Isolation, 1894–1905* (Oxford: Oxford University Press, 2007).

28. Frank F. Wong, "The American Experience in China," *Beloit Magazine* (Winter 1982), 3. See also Jane Hunter, *The Gospel of Gentility* (New Haven, CT: Yale University Press, 1984); Michael Lazich, "American Missionaries and the Opium Trade in Nineteenth Century China," *Journal of World History* 17, no. 2 (June 2007): 197–223; Jennifer Lin, *Shanghai Faithful: Betrayal and Forgiveness in a Chinese Christian Family* (London: Rowman & Littlefield, 2017).

29. Wong, "The American Experience in China," 3.

30. Lee, *At America's Gates*, 89.

31. Lee, *Making of Asian America*, ch. 4.

32. Ibid.

33. There is no close relationship between Wong Kim Ark and Wong Doo Set's brother, Wong Ben Yuk. Their stories bear a resemblance in that both claim to have been born in San Francisco and returned to China as children. Wong Kim Ark claimed birth in San Francisco four years earlier than Wong Ben Yuk.

34. Only fathers, not mothers, transmitted U.S. citizenship to their children born abroad from 1790 to 1934.

35. Mary Wong Palmer is unsure of the parentage of the first son who was brought to the United States, Wong Bok Ngow (a.k.a. Wong Gwong On).

36. Chicago's population was 112,172 in 1860 and 503,185 in 1880. It was 2.1 million by 1910. U.S. Census.

37. McKeown, *Chinese Migrant Networks*, 25.

38. Madeline Y. Hsu, *The Good Immigrants: How the Yellow Peril Became the Model Minority* (Princeton, NJ: Princeton University Press, 2015), 12–17; Ling, *Chinese Chicago*, 173.

39. Document #12, "A Chinese Student Living in the Community," interviewed August 1924, Chicago Research Center, Chicago History Museum.

40. As a prosperous Chinese businessman in Chicago, Wong Doo Set (and his son Charles) can be placed squarely in the conservative camp of Chinese who espoused integration as a means of acceptance in American society. For an excellent analysis of these groups and their efforts to protect Chinese immigrants, see Ling, *Chinese Chicago*, 132–53.

41. Harry Kiang, Table 18, "Distribution of the Chinese Population by Wards in Chicago 1890," compiled from the Eleventh Census of the United States, Chicago Research Center, Chicago History Museum.

42. Grace Krause, "A Cup of Real Chinese Tea: Culinary Adventurism and the Contact Zone at the World's Columbian Exposition, 1893," *Graduate Association for Food Studies* 5, no. 1 (December 11, 2018), https://gradfoodstudies.org/2018/06/01/a -cup-of-real-chinese-tea-culinary-adventurism-and-the-contact-zone-at-the-worlds -columbian-exposition-1893/.

43. Ibid.

44. Kiang, "Distribution of the Chinese Population," 5. A document from 1915 offers 229 I Street in Sacramento as Wong Ben Yuk's place of business as a "Chinese druggist." See 30734/3–23 WONG Ben Yuk file, NARA San Bruno.

45. One document from 1929 lists the address of Wong Ben Yuk's place of business as 146 W. 22nd Street, in Chinatown. October 9, 1929, form in 30734/3–23 WONG Ben Yuk file, NARA San Bruno.

46. Mary Wong Palmer, "Notes from Conversation with Uncle Bob," March 12, 1999. Years earlier Mary had interviewed Albert Wong, who said grandfather's office in Chicago was on Cermak Road, east of Wentworth, four stores down on the north side of the street. Information from Albert Wong interview, June 8, 1991; notes, WFP.

47. Mary Wong Palmer email to Cynthia Wong, which cited her cousin, Susan Toy, March 28, 2009. Claims vary about which of Charles's siblings were his first wife's children, but Susan Toy said Charles had only one full sibling, a sister, WFP.

48. Ibid.

49. "Additional Evidence Interview" (in secondary after denial) for Wong Mun Nging and Wong Mun Bin (Bill and Ben), ages 10 and 12, May 11, 1925, in 30734/3–23 WONG Ben Yuk file, NARA San Bruno.

50. Ibid.

51. Ibid.

52. They both earned a "Proficient+" grade in language in June 1926 after earning a "Failure" in language in January. In contrast to the assumption that primary class sizes were larger in the past, there were only twelve children in the boys' first grade class. Royce School Records, Beloit Historical Society.

53. Fung's children, Alan and Mary, also attended Royce Elementary in the late 1950s and early 1960s. Mary Scholz Hoffert interview, July 15, 2018.

54. Interview documents, September 16, 1931, Wong Mun Soo binder, WFP.

55. Telegram from Harry Hull, Commissioner of Immigration to Immigration Service, October 28, 1931, copy in "Wong Mun Soo Immigration" folder, WFP.

56. Address found on October 9, 1929, form in in 30734/3–23 WONG Ben Yuk file, NARA San Bruno.

57. Mary Wong Palmer, "Notes from Conversation with (surviving twin) Uncle Bob," March 12, 1999, WFP.

58. The death certificate for Wong Bing Yoke stated cause of death as chronic nephritis, an inflammation of the kidney; onset of disease June 1933. His young son had died in March that same year. The certificate lists his year of birth as 1873, a year earlier than other materials for Wong Ben Yuk, which all list 1874. His body was embalmed and "removed" to China. State of California Certificate of Death, WFP. Permit to allow sons to return body to China, April 1934, in WONG Mun Bin file, NARA San Bruno. Notes from conversation with Albert Wong, June 8, 1991, confirmed that Wong Doo Set died of chronic nephritis while awaiting permission to return to China with Ben, Bill, and Bob. Ben and Bob accompanied his remains, leaving May 11, 1934, WFP.

59. Susan Toy remembers going from Hong Kong to Mong Dee for Wong Doo Set's burial as a seven-year-old child. Mary Wong Palmer notes, WFP.

60. This is an assumption. In a 1925 NARA interview of Wong Ben Yuk (a.k.a. Wong Doo Set), he said his father was buried in Dai Hill, his mother in Lai Hill, east of the village. "Additional Evidence Interview," May 11, 1925, in 30734/3–23 WONG Ben Yuk file, NARA San Bruno.

Chapter 2. Immigration and Settlement in Beloit

1. In a December 17, 2009, letter transmitted by the Consulate General for the People's Republic of China in Los Angeles, the Bureau of External Affairs for Overseas Chinese identified Charles as Wong/Huang Guang-Han, WFP.

2. According to Mary Wong Palmer's cousin Susan Toy, Charles's mother died in 1909. Her death would have been in the same time period as the death of Charles's

uncle, second brother Wong Doo Hane. Charles's father's second wife died in 1958 (Yee Shee had visited with her in 1948). See "Family Genealogy" folder, WFP. See also the chart in chapter 1 showing four generations of the Wong family.

3. Wong Soon Pon, Charles's immigration father, testified that "Wong Seung" (Charles) entered the United States with his "brother," Wong Git, who was about a year older than Charles. In 1922, the alleged father said both Wong Git and "Wong Seung" were in Wisconsin. "Wong Soon Pon" folder, WFP.

4. Fourth brother Wong Chow (a.k.a. Wong Doo Sung) arrived in the United States only a few years before Charles, having walked from Mong Dee to Hoi Ping, taken a steamboat to Guangzhou, a boat or train to Hong Kong, and a ship to the United States. When he arrived aboard the SS *Korea*, Wong Chow was detained but filed a writ of habeas corpus regarding his claim to U.S. citizenship birth and was released after one month of detention on May 9, 1903. He had been born in San Francisco on May 15, 1880. Wong Chow died September 28, 1942. His sons are Wong cousins George, Albert, and Kay; his daughter is Susan Wong Toy. Information from Susan Toy to Helen Wong Way, WFP.

5. Preclearance request shows Wong Theong (Charles) to be a cook in Ogden, Utah, as does his Certificate of Identity, November 8, 1915, WFP. Charles's eldest son, Gim Wong, said his father had only lived in Ogden, Chicago, and Beloit. "Wong Family Reminiscences," 1991, WFP.

6. Marion J. Levy, *The Family Revolution in Modern China* (Cambridge, MA: Harvard University Press, 1949), 99.

7. Ibid., 104.

8. Charles's father was almost certainly in Mong Dee for the nuptials. Wong Ben Yuk returned to China in 1908 and died between 1908 and 1912, when Wong Doo Set—Charles's father—landed in the United States using his name. Wong Doo Set returned to China within a month of his 1912 landing and only came back to the United States in 1915. 30734/3–23 WONG Ben Yuk file, NARA San Bruno.

9. The following narrative is speculative and derived from two sources: Annie Cormack, *Chinese Births, Weddings, and Funerals* (Peking, 1923) and reminiscences of a Chinese American woman's conversations with her grandmother, also married in a small village outside Guangzhou in 1913. Jean O'Hara, *Through the Dragon's Gate: Memories of a Hong Kong Childhood* (Cirencester, Gloucestershire: Mereo Books, 2016).

10. Cormack, *Chinese Births, Weddings, and Funerals*, 42. Later in her life, Yee Shee gathered jewelry for her daughters and for her sons to present to their future wives during her 1948 trip to Hong Kong. Mary Wong Palmer interview.

11. "Additional Evidence Interview," May 11, 1925, WONG Ben Yuk file, NARA San Bruno.

12. Immigration records place Charles in Ogden, Utah, in 1915. This may be where he did his apprenticeship as a cook before going back to China to marry in

1913. Wong Soon Pon file, NARA San Bruno. He may have returned to Ogden on his return. Charles's eldest son, Gim Wong, suggested his father feared being drafted in Ogden and disappeared in California during World War I. See "Wong Family Reminiscences," 1991, WFP. Charles headed to San Francisco, possibly to help his father, who had gone to the United States once in 1912 but had left within a month and returned in 1915. 30734/3–23 WONG Ben Yuk file, NARA San Bruno.

13. U.S. Census, 1910 and 1920. Julian and Adele Meyer remained at the same address, 90 Commonwealth Avenue in San Francisco, for years.

14. Letter from the Immigrant Inspector to the Commissioner of Immigration on Angel Island, April 18, 1916, WONG Theong file, NARA San Bruno. This narrative is supported by the reading of these files by Charles's daughter-in-law, Cynthia Wong Stamberger. Cynthia remembers seeing a stamp on a fraud file marked "case closed" after Charles's death. Cynthia Wong Stamberger interview, July 14, 2018, WFP.

15. Gim Wong said in a February 23, 1991, interview that Wong Chow, Albert's father, and his brother started the restaurant in Beloit and that his father, Charles, came to Beloit to work for his uncles, WFP.

16. Wong Hop and Wong Luck were listed in the first entry in the Beloit directory for "Lo Nanking" in 1914. No names were included in subsequent directories until Wong Theong (Charles) was listed in the 1924 directory. However, the 1920 census lists two relatives, Wong Chow (Albert's father) and Lee Yuen (Dok Toy's father), as proprietors of the restaurant. Workers named in the 1920 census are Wong Cheong, Wong Sun, and Wong Doock, ages 21, 30, and 60, respectively. Although family notes do not support this, a newspaper article from 1938 alleged there were five owners: Charles, Don, Att, and two others, Ben and Victor Wong. *Beloit Daily News*, July 16, 1938. Family notes suggest the owners from 1920 forward were Charles and his father's third, fourth, and sixth brothers, Wong Doo Yee, Wong Doo Sung, and Wong Doo Foo. Mary Wong Palmer, WFP.

17. Beatrice McKenzie, "Beloit Wisconsin 1896–1914," paper presented and published as part of a conference in economics and globalization headlined by Dani Rodrik, professor of international political economy at the Kennedy School of Government, Harvard University. For a recent examination of Britain's role in colonial and global history, see Roland Wenzelhuemer, *Connecting the Nineteenth-Century World: The Telegraph and Globalization* (Cambridge: Cambridge University Press, 2012). See also Jeffry Frieden, *Global Capitalism: Its Rise and Fall in the Twentieth Century* (New York: W. W. Norton, 2006).

18. U.S. Census.

19. U.S. Census.

20. "Americanization" memorandum detailed Fairbanks, Morse and Company's diverse workforce in July 1923: 229 Black workers, 185 Italians, 77 Greeks, 64 Germans, 126 Danish/Swedes/Norwegians, and 64 English/Scots/Irish. "Weaver History," in "Fairbanks Morse" folder, Beloit College Archives.

21. "Night School Filling Need of Foreigners," *Beloit Daily News*, December 10, 1915.

22. Isabel Wilkerson, *The Warmth of Other Suns: The Epic Story of America's Great Migration* (New York: Random House, 2011), 253, 183–84.

23. Velma Fern Bell, "The Negro in Beloit and Madison, Wisconsin" (master's thesis, University of Wisconsin–Madison, 1933), 25. Beloit College Archives.

24. It is unknown what the Wongs offered, whether cash, gold or silver, or a private loan. Rock County Register of Deeds, Rock County, Wisconsin. Between 1926 and 1940 the Olsons lived with their adult son, Oscar, in a home at 1314 W. Merrill, two blocks away from the Wongs. Beloit City Directories, U.S. Census.

25. *Book of Beloit II* (Beloit, WI: Beloit Daily News, 1986), Beloit College Archives, 150.

26. Ibid., 168–69.

27. Frederick W. Job, "A Tale of Two Cities," *Public Policy*, April 2, 1904, 165.

28. Katherine Leonard Turner, *How the Other Half Ate: A History of Working-Class Meals at the Turn of the Century* (Berkeley: University of California Press, 2014). See especially chapter 3, page 59.

29. Sanborn Perris maps: 1896, 1902, 1908, 1915. Available online at Wisconsin Historical Society.

30. See Beloit city directories, 1905 and 1908, Beloit Historical Society.

31. "Front man" comes from notes Charles left about his position at the restaurant. Relationships with Beloit elite included the Neeses (iron manufacturing), the Freemans (shoe manufacturing), the McGavocks (ice, lumber, and fuel company), and the Stewarts (greenhouse owner). Charles would visit William and Lottie Stewart and Lucien and Emma Rea on Sundays, and for years after Charles's death the Stewarts sent flowers to the Wongs on special holidays. "Wong Family Reminiscences," 1991, WFP; Fung Wong Scholz interview, March 13, 2021.

32. "Wong Family Reminiscences," 1991, WFP.

33. Son George said at different times his father owned a Model T Ford and a Graham Paige car. George Ham Wong interviewed by Mary Wong Palmer, September 17, 2010, WFP. Gim said when Charles purchased the Graham Paige in about 1930, "He didn't even know how to drive it" and nearly hit the maple tree by the house. "Wong Family Reminiscences," 1991, WFP.

34. Fung Wong Scholz interview, April 3, 2018.

35. Ibid.

36. Fung Wong Scholz and John Wong still attend Sun Valley Presbyterian Church in Beloit, where West Side Presbyterian moved in 1963.

37. Fung Wong Scholz interview, March 20, 2019.

38. "Wong Chow" folder, WFP.

39. Frank's notes, found on his desk after his death, said Father decided to stay in the United States after the Japanese took over in 1931. Mother decided to stay (after

his death) and received a small inheritance from Western Title Company for $1,500. Because Charles had had no will, 50 percent of the inheritance went to Yee Shee and 50 percent to their children in separate bank accounts that Yee Shee controlled. Mary remembers accompanying her mother to the bank and translating for her.

40. Charles owned one property on Hennessy Road and one on Egg Street. Wong Chow owned two properties on Hennessy. The two shared ownership of another property on Hennessy Road.

41. Newspaper accounts from *Racine Journal-Times*, July 16, 1938; *Wisconsin State Journal*, July 16, 1938; *Dubuque Telegraph Herald*, July 16, 1938; *Appleton Post-Crescent*, July 16, 1938; *Ironwood Daily Globe*, July 16, 1938; *Oshkosh Northwestern*, July 16, 1938. Letter from cousin James Wong, Terry Lee's brother, to Helen Wong Way, September 12, 1979, Bellevue, Washington, says the family knew it to be an argument between the two men, WFP.

42. Descriptions of what actually happened differ. Some accounts, including the family's, say that Don went to his lodging to get the gun; the newspaper says he was carrying the gun. It is possible his lawyer encouraged him to say he was carrying the gun to shore up the insanity claim. "Chinese Confesses Killing His Kinsman," *Appleton Post-Crescent*, July 16, 1938. Some reports say Charles was shot five times. See *Wisconsin State Journal*, November 23, 1938. The death certificate states as cause of death "hemorrhage and shock resultant of five bullet wounds" and mentions the wounds are to the body and face. State of Wisconsin Department of Health Bureau of Vital Statistics, WFP.

43. A later newspaper report indicated that Don's son lived in Cincinnati, Ohio, and that two other sons and a daughter lived with his wife in China.

44. *Beloit Daily News*, July 16, 1938.

45. The newspaper account states that Don Wong went to the Beloit Hospital with a four-inch gash over his right eye and a five-inch gash on his left forearm. *Beloit Daily News*, July 16, 1938.

46. *Oshkosh Northwester*, July 16, 1938.

47. "Beloit Chinese Gets 14–20 Years for Slaying Pal," *Wisconsin State Journal*, November 23, 1938. *La Crosse Tribune* and *Leader Press*, November 23, 1938. The family believes if Yee Shee had testified against Don Wong, he would have been sentenced to death. Kathryn Wong's husband, Albert, worked with Don in Cincinnati, Ohio. She remembered Don's terrible temper. Although Don promised Albert a 50 percent share in the restaurant, Albert left the job because of Don's temper. Kathryn Wong to Mary Wong Palmer, WFP.

48. 1940 U.S. Census.

Chapter 3. Surviving and Thriving in Beloit

1. Yee Shee's parents were YEE Thien Wu (a.k.a. YEE Sung Wah, father) and LIU Moi Han (a.k.a. FAM Nan Wah, mother). "History of Yee Shee Gok by Her

Daughter Mary Wong Palmer," 2016, revised 2018, WFP. See also Mary Wong Palmer notes from conversation with maternal cousin Soo Sum Yee, February 27, 1993, WFP.

2. Chen Lai is a professor of philosophy at Tsinghua University, Beijing. He examines the development of Confucianism in China in the twentieth century, dividing the century into four periods, the late Qing/early Republic (1901–1911), the New Culture Movement (1915–1919), 1949–1976, and the twenty years following the end of the Cultural Revolution (1976–1996). Chen Lai, "A Century of Confucianism," in *Voices from the Chinese Century: Public Intellectual Debate from Contemporary China,* ed. Timothy Cheek, David Ownby, and Joshua Fogel (New York: Columbia University Press, 2014), 306–17, 308.

3. For other works on Chinese women who immigrated to the United States, see Zeng Jifen Nie, *Testimony of a Confucian Woman: The Autobiography of Mrs. Nie Zeng Jifen, 1852–1942* (Athens: University of Georgia Press, 1993); Pang-Mei Natasha Chang, *Bound Feet and Western Dress: A Memoir* (New York: Doubleday, 1996); and oral histories contained in Judy Yung, *Chinese Women of America: A Pictorial History* (Seattle: University of Washington Press, 1986).

4. Far from being an unchanging set of requirements, Confucian virtues were defined and deployed in different situations for different reasons. The historical and cultural context within which virtues were deployed—having to work harder to overcome racial discrimination as racialized immigrants in the United States, for example—is significant.

5. Yung, *Chinese Women of America*, 10. In addition to offering a much fuller discussion on the topic, Yung quotes a Chinese proverb, "Eighteen gifted daughters are not equal to one lame son" (13). In *Confucianism and Women: A Philosophical Interpretation* (Albany: SUNY Press, 2006), Li-Hsiang Lisa Rosenlee helpfully explores the philosophy of the Confucian cultural and social practices in pre-Republican China, elucidating expectations and values for women and for men.

6. Yee Shee's children and grandchildren remarked on her even temperament and good cheer. Her husband's younger brother, Bob Wong, paid her the ultimate compliment about her time in the village in the ten years after her marriage by saying she was described as a "good girl." Mary Wong Palmer takes that to mean Yee Shee behaved correctly by village standards: worked hard and was uncomplaining. Charles's family recognized Yee Shee's value in their gifts of jade and gold jewelry to Yee Shee's family as a largely symbolic "bride price." Yee Shee divided these items among her children before she died. Mary Wong Palmer interview.

7. Because photographs are human constructions, they are emblematic of the values of the dominant social class rather than representations of reality. Laura Wexler advises to separate out the "semantic units" (selection of subject and setting, composition) of the photo before critically examining possible meanings. Laura Wexler, *Tender Violence: Domestic Vision in an Age of U.S. Imperialism* (Chapel Hill: University of North Carolina Press, 2000), 55.

8. Mary Wong Palmer's notes on the photo say that her grandmother was around fifty at the time, WFP.

9. When he arrived back in the United States, Charles claimed he had one son. No family member has had information about a possible elder brother since then. Mary Wong Palmer interview.

10. Notes from conversation between Yee Soo Sum (Yee Shee's niece who came to live with her husband in San Francisco in 1956) and Mary Wong Palmer, February 27, 1993, WFP.

11. Mary Wong Palmer, "Notes from Conversation with (surviving twin) Uncle Bob," March 12, 1999, WFP.

12. Huping Ling argues that prostitution was part of the global movement of Chinese laborers. For men, prostitution filled in for an absent family life and offered relief and recreation in their otherwise dull and hard-working daily lives. Women were purchased or duped into marrying a smuggler in China who then sold them to individuals as concubines or to brothel owners as sex workers. There were no professional Chinese prostitutes before the 1920s and even after that, prostitution was a small, unorganized, and unprofitable business. Ling, *Chinese Chicago*, 91–93.

13. Yung, *Chinese Women of America*, 15.

14. Hong Fan, *Footbinding, Feminism, and Freedom: The Liberation of Women's Bodies in Modern China* (Ilford, Essex: Frank Cass Publishers, 1997), 78–80. See also Pang-Mei Natasha Chang, *Bound Feet and Western Dress*. Judy Yung compares the practice to the wearing of corsets in nineteenth-century American society (*Chinese Women of America*, 13).

15. Wang Ping, "Footbinding and the Cult of the Exemplary Woman," in *Aching for Beauty: Footbinding in China* (Minneapolis: University of Minnesota Press, 2000), 55–78, 69.

16. Sanjay Seth, "Nationalism, Modernity, and the 'Woman Question' in India and China," *The Journal of Asian Studies* 72, no. 2 (May 2013): 273–97, 282.

17. Interviews with Fung Wong Scholz and with Lani Way, July 2018.

18. The Immigration Act of 1924. These reasons are explored by Him Mark Lai in his *Autobiography of a Chinese American Historian*, 18–20. Him Mark Lai's father also brought his wife to the United States by first-class passage in 1923 "so as to facilitate their entry into America."

19. Admiral Oriental Line passenger list, WFP.

20. The *Olympian* left Seattle daily at 9:30 a.m. and on the third day would arrive in Milwaukee at 9:10 a.m. and in Chicago at 11:30 a.m. Charles and Yee Shee would have easily caught a connecting train to Beloit from either Milwaukee or Chicago. See Chicago, Milwaukee, and St. Paul Railway advertisement in *Seattle Star*, December 6, 1922, in Library of Congress, https://chroniclingamerica.loc.gov/lccn/sn8709 3407/1922-12-06/ed-1/seq-10/, and "The Olympian en route Chicago to Seattle and Tacoma (1911)," https://content.libraries.wsu.edu/digital/collection/maps/id/362/.

21. As an industrial powerhouse with good schools, Beloit was one northern destination for Black migrants. Wilkerson, *The Warmth of Other Suns*, 243. For explorations of relations between the races in this era in larger cities, see Albert M. Camarillo, "Navigating Segregated Life in America's Racial Borderhoods, 1910s–1950s," *Journal of American History* 100, no. 3 (December 2013): 645–62.

22. U.S. Census.

23. "Too Much Energy Is Needed in Colored Skin, Savant Says," *Beloit Daily News*, July 23, 1923.

24. *Beloit Daily News* shoe polish ad April 20, 1915; Chi-namel ad April 2, 1915; Jap Rose soap, October 20, 1915; Beloit College Archives.

25. "Chinese Will Try Christian Religion, Dr. J. Taylor States: Will Be Permitted to Interpret Religion in Its Own Way," *Beloit Daily News*, July 25, 1923.

26. The first Chinese student at Beloit College was C. Y. Tang, class of 1918. "Fridays with Fred: The Beloit College Chinese Students Club," https://www.beloit .edu/live/news/620-fridays-with-fred-the-beloit-college-chinese.

27. Hsu, *The Good Immigrants*, 41–43. Arthur H. Smith was a missionary in China for fifty-four years beginning in 1872. https://www.beloit.edu/archives/documents/ archival_collections/alumni/arthur_smith/.

28. See "Fridays with Fred: The Beloit College Chinese Students Club."

29. Ibid.

30. Charles Antonsen, Swedish immigrant, and his wife Emma, second-generation German, lived at 1115 Merrill Street. Frank and Mary Seach, in a multigenerational household at 1109 Merrill Street, emigrated from Hungary. Frank Anderson, second-generation Swedish, was married to Swedish immigrant Laura, at 1103 Merrill Street. Linda Wolfe, across the street on Lincoln Avenue, was second-generation German. Lloyd and Grace Root were second-generation Danish. An elderly couple two doors down from the Wongs, Alex and Bertha Anderson, were Norwegian immigrants. U.S. Census.

31. Mary Wong Palmer, "Memories of Mother," in "Yee Shee" folder, WFP.

32. Helen Hong Wong (no relation), in Yung, *Chinese Women of America*, 44.

33. Rosenlee, *Confucianism and Women*, 124.

34. Iris Chang, *The Chinese in America: A Narrative History* (New York: Viking, 2003), 174–75. This quote was heard in several of Yee Shee's grandchildren's interviews. See, for example, John Wong interview, April 16, 2019, WFP.

35. They lived at 1029 Lincoln Avenue. In the 1930 census and 1933 and 1936 City Directories, the husband, a farm laborer and then a barber, was in the household. He was no longer in the household in the 1940 census. U.S. Census, Beloit City Directories, Beloit Historical Society.

36. https://www.statelinefamilyservices.org/about_us.

37. Fung Wong Scholz interview, April 3, 2018.

38. Detail from Frank's undated notes, found in his desk after his death. Frank's notes said his mother sold their share in the restaurant in 1938 for $1,500. Western Title Company distributed the money to Yee Shee and the children, and she used the money in their accounts to buy food in subsequent years. "Frank Wong" folder, WFP.

39. "Hong Kong Property" folder, WFP.

40. See 1976–1977 exchange of letters between the Chief Estate Surveyor and Wong Kwong Hon (Charles Wong). Gim acted on Charles's behalf in the negotiations, in "Hong Kong Property" folder, WFP. For more information, see "Wong Family Reminiscences," 1991, WFP.

41. Because she was unable to visit Guangdong, Yee Shee sent money to her father-in-law's widow and to her own sister to visit her in Hong Kong in 1948. Yee Shee also met Wong Chow's daughter, Susan Toy, for the first time, as well as his son, Albert's wife Kathryn, and her daughter Gloria, all of whom eventually came to live in Wisconsin. Mary Wong Palmer history, 4, WFP.

42. Marjorie M. Van Galder, *Taming the Blue: The Thrills and Challenges of One Man's Journey in Private Aviation* (Plum Tree Publications, 1991). See also "Wong Family Reminiscences," 1991, WFP.

43. Yung, *Chinese Women of America*, 10.

44. Ibid., 11. See discussion of widow fidelity and integrity in Li-Hsiang Rosenlee, *Confucianism and Women*, 130–38. Remarriage, which could only have been accomplished with familial involvement, could have meant loss of the right of her children to inherit their father's property as well as loss of custody of the children.

45. Frank relayed this story with characteristic modesty in a letter to Mary congratulating her for winning a scholarship to University of Wisconsin–Madison. He wrote: "Your class scholarships have relegated ours to obscurity! I'm glad." Frank Wong letter to Mary Wong, May 13, 1955, WFP.

46. Mary Wong Palmer interview, March 9, 2021.

47. Naturalization Certificate, Yee Shee WONG, WFP.

48. Wendy Wong Dereix interview, July 28, 2018; David Wong interview, June 18, 2018.

49. Cathy Wong Ring interview, July 14, 2018.

50. John Wong interview, April 16, 2019, WFP.

51. Mary Wong Palmer, history, 6, WFP.

Chapter 4. Family, Work, and Wartime Service

1. Sucheng Chan, "Race, Ethnic Culture, and Gender in the Construction of Identities among Second Generation Chinese Americans, 1880s to 1930s," in *Claiming America*, ed. K. Scott Wong and Sucheng Chan (Philadelphia, PA: Temple University Press, 1998), 127–63, 157.

2. Ibid., 139.

3. "Wong Family Reminiscences," 1991, WFP. Gim and Fung also shared that on Saturdays their mother "forced [them] to sit there and read and then write [Chinese]" with rice paper, ink, and brush. The other kids were not required to learn to write Chinese.

4. All of the children suffered the taunt "Chin Chin Chinaman" from neighborhood kids. Gim said neighbor children threw rocks. "Wong Family Reminiscences," 1991, WFP. Fung reported that children threw rocks at her until she threatened to bring her step-uncles out. Fung Wong Scholz interview, April 3, 2018. As a mother, Fung defended her very upset daughter when another child called her "Chink," marching down to the child's house to let her mother know this was unacceptable. Mary Scholz Hoffert interview, July 15, 2018.

5. When his father died, Gim led the family; the third of the "Three Obediences" was for a Chinese woman to obey her eldest son when widowed. Yung, *Chinese Women of America*, 10.

6. Gim Wong Beloit College application, 1947, Beloit College Archives.

7. 1942 Beloit High School Yearbook, Beloit Historical Society.

8. Gim Wong Beloit College application.

9. Ibid.

10. Wendy Wong Dereix interview, July 14, 2018. See also Palmer interview of Gim Wong, 2010, WFP.

11. Palmer interview of Gim Wong. Gim's sister Mary remembers Gim said he was not on the frontlines because he might have been mistaken for a Japanese enemy soldier. Gim likely served in a segregated unit. For information about anti-Asian racism and the existence of segregated units in China during World War II, see K. Scott Wong, *Americans First: Chinese Americans and the Second World War* (Cambridge, MA: Harvard University Press, 2005).

12. Essay for admission in fall, 1947, Gim Wong Beloit College application, Beloit College Archives.

13. Mary Wong Palmer notes, "Yee Shee," WFP.

14. Theresa Lee Yih interview, November 2019.

15. Although the deed remained in Charles's name, Gim acted in his father's place. Deed of sale document, "Hong Kong Properties," WFP.

16. Mary Wong Palmer interview, June 19, 2018.

17. Peggy Pascoe, *What Comes Naturally: Miscegenation Law and the Making of Race in America* (New York: Oxford University Press, 2010).

18. Harry Wong interview, June 2, 2018. Fung Wong Scholz interview, February 27, 2019. Notes left by Frank Wong, 1995, in possession of Mary Wong Palmer.

19. Gender balance among Chinese Americans changed dramatically, from 27:1 in 1890 to 7:1 in 1920 to 2:1 in 1960. However, many in the latter group had immigrated as wives and fiancées of American GIs after World War II, so they cannot be counted among eligible partners for second-generation Chinese American men. In

1960, moreover, nearly half—49.6 percent—of all Chinese and Chinese Americans lived in California. Ellen Wu, *The Color of Success* (Princeton, NJ: Princeton University Press, 2014), 145–46.

20. John Wong interview, April 16, 2019, WFP.

21. "Marion Erdman Becomes Bride of Gim C. Wong," news clipping marked June 28, 1954, in Gim Wong file, Beloit College Archives.

22. Fung Wong Scholz interview, March 20, 2019.

23. "Gim Wong" folder, Beloit Historical Society.

24. Author unknown, "Gim Wong" folder, Beloit Historical Society.

25. Interviews with Wendy Wong Dereix, July 14, 2018, and John Wong, April 16, 2019.

26. Sucheng Chan, "Race, Ethnic Culture, and Gender," 141.

27. Gender historian Judy Yung describes her own inspiration coming from Jade Snow Wong's autobiography *Fifth Chinese Daughter* in "In Our Own Words," 114.

28. "Fungie" served as junior class secretary, senior class treasurer, yearbook staff, Delphic Lyceum representative, forensics, secretary-treasurer of Thalian, and other clubs. Her classmates called her "an outstanding student." 1944 Beloit High School Yearbook, Beloit Historical Society.

29. In cities with larger Chinese American populations, most Chinese girls were waitresses and garment workers, and some worked as maids in private homes after high school. "It was the war that opened the door to better-paying jobs for Chinese American women. Aimei Chen, who came to the United States shortly after she was born, had grown up in a small Chinese community in Stockton. Before the war, she had worked as a waitress in a Chinese café while attending junior college. Some Caucasian girls her age got jobs in local dime stores, ice cream parlors, and department stores. Aimei, however, had never applied for those jobs because she knew no Chinese would be hired." Xiaojian Zhao, "Chinese American Women Defense Workers in World War II," *California History* 75, no. 2 (Summer 1996): 138–53, 146–47.

30. Velma Bell, a Black woman who graduated at the top of her class at Beloit Memorial High School in 1926, reported to Beloit College, which she attended, that "housework" was the only work available to girls of her race in summer 1929. Fred Burwell, "Fridays with Fred: Velma Bell and Beloit," January 13, 2011, https://www.beloit.edu/live/news/626-fridays-with-fred-velma-bell-and-beloit. Other young Black women and men who grew up in Beloit similarly found better opportunities elsewhere.

31. Transcript of oral history conducted for Cadet Nurse program and book, March 4, 1995, WFP.

32. Allan Berubet, *Coming Out Under Fire: The History of Gay Men and Women in World War II*, Twentieth Anniversary Edition (Chapel Hill: University of North Carolina Press, 2010).

33. Fung Wong Scholz interview, March 20, 2019.

34. Fung Wong, Cadet Nurse program, March 4, 1995, WFP.

35. At the time, nursing degree candidates did not earn a bachelor's degree. Fung and her roommate Alice wanted to get their bachelor's degrees to qualify as supervisors of surgery. Fung Wong Scholz interview, April 3, 2018.

36. Interview with Fung Wong Scholz, Mary Scholz Hoffert, and Cherie Scholz Baker, February 27, 2019.

37. Young Chinese and Chinese American men faced daunting discrimination in the job market in the 1940s and 1950s. See Ling, *Chinese Chicago*, 158–59.

38. Fung Wong Scholz interview, March 20, 2019.

39. Alan Scholz interview, May 15, 2019.

40. Though the ratio of Chinese men to Chinese women had improved greatly from 20:1 in 1900, it was still considerable at 3:1 in 1940. Xiaojian Zhao, "Chinese American Women Defense Workers," 142. See also Ling, *Chinese Chicago*, 207.

41. Mary Scholz Hoffert visited Yee Shee often in grade school. She loved her grandmother and being at the house, with particular memories of the eight-by-six root cellar in the basement where Yee Shee kept herbal medicines on shelves that were labeled in Chinese. It smelled like a Chinese pharmacy. Mary Scholz Hoffert interview, July 15, 2018.

42. Interviews with Alan Scholz (May 15, 2019), Mary Scholz Hoffert (July 15, 2018, February 26, 2019), and Cherie Scholz Baker (February 26, 2019).

43. Mary Scholz Hoffert interview, July 15, 2018.

44. Fung Wong Scholz reminiscences, included in "George Wong 70th Birthday Scrapbook," November 6, 1998. In possession of Lisa Wong Fortsch. See also "Wong Family Reminiscences," 1991, WFP.

45. Cathy Wong Ring interview, July 14, 2018.

46. Mary Wong Palmer interview of George Wong, September 17, 2020, WFP.

47. 1946 Beloit High School Yearbook, Beloit Historical Society.

48. Mary Wong Palmer interview of George Wong, September 17, 2010, WFP. James H. McNeel was principal of Beloit Memorial High School from 1913 to 1946, so George Wong graduated the year McNeel retired. Fran Fruzen and Melissa Badger, eds., "History of Beloit Schools," School District of Beloit, January 24, 2013, https://www.sdb.k12.wi.us/.

49. George Ham Wong application folder, Beloit College Archives.

50. Mary Wong Palmer interview of George Wong, September 17, 2010, WFP.

51. George Q. Flynn, "The Draft and College Deferments during the Korean War," *The Historian* 50, no. 3 (May 1988): 369–85.

52. I. M. McQuiston, "History of the Reserves since the Second World War," *Military Affairs* 17, no. 1 (Spring 1953): 23–27.

53. Ibid.

54. Mary Wong Palmer interview of George Wong, September 17, 2010, WFP.

55. *Beloit Daily News* clipping, dated Summer 1951, George Wong file, Beloit College Archives.

56. Lisa Wong Fortsch interview, June 18, 2018.

57. Mary Wong Palmer interview of George Wong, September 17, 2010, WFP.

58. George converted to Catholicism in 1977. David Wong interview, June 18, 2018.

59. Undated letter from George to Joyce, written as he was heading to Korea, 1952. Written on stationery from Hotel Sir Francis, Powell at Sutter, San Francisco. In possession of Lisa Wong Fortsch.

60. Lisa Wong Fortsch recollections, in "George Wong 70th Birthday Scrapbook," November 6, 1998.

61. One assignment was as general manager for the Wheeler Division of Beloit Corporation in Kalamazoo, Michigan, where his sister Mary and family were also living. The two families got together on Sundays and reestablished a close connection. Mary Wong Palmer interview.

62. David Wong interview, June 18, 2018. See also https://www.tributearchive.com/obituaries/2802775/George-H-Wong.

63. Bill Wong, "In Honor of an Electrical Engineer," March 18, 2021, *Electronic Design*, https://www.electronicdesign.com/technologies/embedded-revolution/article/21802798/in-honor-of-an-electrical-engineer.

64. George and his family lived in West Chester, Pennsylvania, for two stints, from 1960 to 1969 and as general manager of the plastics facility in the Downingtown plant from 1971 to 1975.

65. Mary Wong Palmer reminiscences, in "George Wong 70th Birthday Scrapbook," 1998.

66. Although her children are not certain, Yee Shee may have brought cash back from rent from the Hong Kong property to purchase this house. After Yee Shee's death, Mary found secret pockets sewn into coats and dresses for safeguarding money. Mary Wong Palmer interview.

67. Second son Robert Charles died of a heart condition as an infant. https://www.tributearchive.com/obituaries/2802775/George-H-Wong.

68. Cathy Wong Ring painted Yee Shee's house with her brother David in the summer after her freshman year of high school. Interviews with Cathy, July 14, 2018, and David, June 18, 2018. Warm relationships described in Alan Scholz, David Wong, Rick Wong, John Wong, Lani Way, Lori Way Galloway, Jon Way interviews, among others. The proximity also allowed those grandchildren to get to know each other. Mary Scholz Hoffert interview, July 15, 2018.

69. Mary Wong Palmer reminiscences, 2011, WFP.

70. Bill Wong, undated statement (c. May 2018) in possession of Lisa Wong Fortsch. At the 2015 Wong family reunion in Milwaukee, more than fifty relatives made the two-hour trip to visit George and Joyce at their retirement home in Geneva,

Illinois, "a symbol of the strong Wong family bond instilled in each one of us, and always modeled by George and his siblings." https://www.tributearchive.com/obit uaries/2802775/George-H-Wong.

71. Cathy Wong Ring interview, July 13, 2019.

72. Ibid.

73. Bill Wong taught these skills to his own children, all of whom became engineers. Wong, *Electronic Design*, 2.

74. David Wong interview, June 18, 2018.

75. Cathy Wong Ring interview, July 14, 2018.

76. David Wong interview, June 18, 2018. David credits his dad's guidance for helping him stay out of trouble as a teen, secure a four-year Beloit Corporation scholarship, and select chemical engineering as a field.

77. Eulogy from Lisa Wong Fortsch at George Wong's funeral, 2015. Statement in possession of Lisa Wong Fortsch.

Chapter 5. Part of a National Community

1. Adjectives listed in "Gim Wong" folder, Beloit Historical Society. Grand-children Cherie Scholz Baker, Lisa Wong Fortsch, and John Wong named the values Yee Shee instilled in her children and grandchildren in 2013: "Hard work, respect, patience, resourcefulness, education, and family." "Grandma's Candy Dish" in "Re-union Materials" in possession of Lisa Wong Fortsch.

2. All of the children suffered the taunt "Chin Chin Chinaman" from neighbor-hood kids. Fung and Harry each reported an episode in school where a teacher pre-vented them (Fung) from winning a prize because she had already won or changed the prize (Harry) to a nonmonetary one. Mary and Harry both said their peers did not discriminate against them in Beloit. Several of their nieces and nephews, particularly those who grew up in the Midwest, spoke of experiencing racism as children. See inter-views with Lisa Wong Fortsch (June 18, 2018) and Mary Scholz Hoffert (July 15, 2018).

3. The Wong siblings' reputations were built on achievement in academics and extracurricular activities, including elected office. Racism affected them in dating and marriage. All three daughters dated white peers in the high school with different out-comes (two breakups over race after high school and one marriage in spite of racial difference). Whether the Wong brothers were immature or were found unsuitable by white girls or their families in high school, they had dates for dances but only began dating steadily in college. Three of the four younger siblings married Asian Ameri-can partners. Interviews with Fung Wong Scholz (April 13, 2018), Harry Wong (June 2, 2018), Mary Wong Palmer (June 2010), Wendy Wong Dereix (July 14, 2018), and Lisa Wong Fortsch (June 18, 2018).

4. They were in student government (elected positions), service organizations (international/red cross, ROTC, and the Y), academic honor clubs (NHS, Latin club, literary societies), and social organizations. Two were editors of the yearbook. They

worked on the newspaper. Beloit High School Yearbooks, 1942, 1944, 1946, 1949, 1951, 1953, 1955, Beloit Historical Society.

5. Helen Wong Way letters to Mary and David, to Mother, and to Fung, 1955–1980, in WFP.

6. "Top Girls State Officers Go to Capitol," *Wisconsin State Journal*, June 30, 1948, WFP. Lani Way interview, July 2018.

7. Mary Wong Palmer interview, April 2019.

8. Lani Way interview, July 2018.

9. Mary Wong Palmer interview, June 19, 2018.

10. Letter from Helen Wong to Mary Wong, August 25, 1955, WFP.

11. Helen's experiences in Washington, DC, include descriptions of joyful times as well, including a beach outing with Bryan and another couple where the foursome played music, sang, and danced until 1:30 a.m. Letter from Helen Wong to Mary Wong, August 29, 1955, WFP.

12. Letter from Frank Wong to Mary Wong Palmer, April 19, 1971, WFP.

13. Lani Way interview, July 2018.

14. Scraps of paper have lists of purchases and costs for the wedding. "Helen" folder, WFP.

15. The frugality of the first and second generations of Wongs was mentioned by many of Yee Shee's grandchildren, some of whom had adopted that value for themselves. See Cathy Wong Ring interview, July 14, 2021, WFP.

16. Kimberlé Crenshaw explained that Black women sometimes experienced discrimination like white women and sometimes like Black men, but most often they experienced a double discrimination from their gender and race. "Demarginalizing the Intersection of Race and Sex: A Black Feminist Critique of Antidiscrimination Doctrine, Feminist Theory and Antiracist Politics," *University of Chicago Legal Forum* 1 (1989): 139–67. For a more recent examination of intersectionality, see Devon Carbado, "Colorblind Intersectionality," *Signs: Journal of Women in Culture and Society* 38, no. 4 (2013): 811–45.

17. Jennifer Ho, "Identity," in *Keywords for Asian American Studies*, ed. Cathy Schlung-Vials, Linda Trinh Vo, and K. Scott Wong (New York: New York University Press, 2015), 135–37, 137.

18. Letter from Helen Wong (Washington, DC) to Mary Wong (Beloit; Mary was entering university), August 29, 1955.

19. Lani Way interview, July 2018.

20. Ibid.

21. Eulogy from Mary Wong Palmer at Helen Way's funeral, 1984, "Helen" folder, WFP.

22. See Helen's letters to Mary Wong Palmer, WFP. She learned, for example, that their mother's father had been an only child, one of only a handful of facts we have about Yee Shee's family.

23. Scholars agree that Asian and Black Americans have been racialized in U.S. history relative to each other. Michael Omi and Howard Winant, in *Racial Formation in the United States from the 1960s to the 1990s*, 2nd ed. (New York: Routledge, 1994), suggest Asian Americans are situated between white and Black Americans on a single social hierarchy. In "Imagining Race and Nation in Multiculturalist America," *Ethnic and Racial Studies* 27, no. 6 (2004): 987–1005, Claire Jean Kim sees Asian Americans as providing a third axis in racial triangulation of Asian, Black, and white Americans. In contrast, Xiaofeng Stephanie Da persuasively argues that, rather than seeing Asian Americans as a midpoint between Black and white America or as a leg of a racial triangle, they are situated on the marginal ends of a spectrum, which allows for continued hegemony of white Americans. Xiaofeng Stephanie Da, "Education and Labor Relations: Asian Americans and Blacks as Pawns in the Furtherance of White Hegemony," *Michigan Journal of Race and Law* 13 (2007): 308–35.

24. See also Lucas W. Knowles, "Beloit Wisconsin and the Great Migration: The Role of Industry, Individuals, and Family in the Founding of Beloit's Black Community, 1914–55" (master's thesis, University of Wisconsin–Eau Claire, 2010).

25. Joe William Trotter Jr., *Black Milwaukee: The Making of an Industrial Proletariat, 1915–45*, 2nd ed. (Champaign: University of Illinois Press, 2007), 47, 164.

26. Harry Wong interview, June 2, 2018.

27. Gim Wong said in an interview in 1991 that Harry was the one who always got into trouble and, because of the drinking and late nights, the family was concerned Harry would not amount to anything. "Wong Family Reminiscences," 1991, WFP.

28. People with different ethnic origins—Japanese American, Filipino American, Chinese American, among others—comprise the racial category of Asian American. See Rick Burns, "Ethnicity," in *Keywords for Asian American Studies*, ed. Cathy Schlung-Vials, Linda Trinh Vo, and K. Scott Wong (New York: New York University Press, 2015).

29. Because Japan was an enemy of both China and the United States and because of the very brutal way that Japan had occupied China before and during World War II, many Chinese and Chinese Americans had antipathy toward Japanese and Japanese Americans until after the war. For their part, Japanese Americans had been relegated to concentration camps in the mainland United States (though Japanese in Hawaii were spared that fate). A domestic campaign during the war sought to teach non-Asian Americans how to distinguish between "your [Chinese] friends" and "the Japs." Thus, Yee Shee may have been concerned about Jean's ethnic background while Jean's parents were likely concerned about her safety and distance from them. See Scott Wong, "From Pariah to Paragon: Shifting Images of Chinese Americans during World War II," in *Chinese Americans and the Politics of Race and Culture*, ed. Sucheng Chan and Madeline Hsu (Philadelphia, PA: Temple University Press, 2008), 153–72, 156.

30. It later became clear she had just got off a series of flights from Hawaii to Madison, including a red eye flight to Los Angeles. Harry Wong interview, June 2, 2018.

31. Real estate brokers and developers advanced restrictive covenants to prevent African American and Asian entry into white neighborhoods in Salt Lake City after a 1917 Supreme Court case (*Buchanan v. Warley*) outlawed racial zoning. Other cities that used restrictive covenants extensively included New York City, Chicago, St. Louis, Detroit, Milwaukee, and different cities in California, including Berkeley. Federal home lending practices supported these discriminatory practices. Richard Brooks and Carol Rose, "The Calculus of Covenants," in *Saving the Neighborhood* (Cambridge, MA: Harvard University Press, 2013), 106.

32. Harry C. Wong, "Anesthesiology," in *Medicine in the Beehive State, 1940–1990*, ed. Henry Plenk (Salt Lake City: Utah Medical Society, 1992), 439–52, 447.

33. Ibid., 439–52.

34. Frank Wong letter to Mary Wong Palmer, July 19, 1963, WFP.

35. Frank Wong letter to Mary Wong, June 2, 1956, WFP.

36. Frank Wong letter to Mary Wong Palmer, April 14, 1968, WFP. Frank reported with satisfaction that George's family was happy.

37. Frank studied language and classical Chinese texts (texts on Confucius, on Buddhism, Laozi's *Tao Te Ching*, and *Shi-jing, the First Book of Songs*) with Mrs. Yeh, an older woman who had escaped Beijing in 1949. The Stanford language school was the best place to learn Mandarin Chinese and study literature when China was closed to Americans and much literature was destroyed during the Cultural Revolution. Cynthia Wong Stamberger email to Mary Wong Palmer, May 29, 2018, WFP.

38. Cynthia Wong Stamberger interview, July 14, 2018, WFP.

39. Cynthia Wong Stamberger email to Mary Wong Palmer, May 29, 2018, WFP.

40. Cynthia Wong Stamberger said they enjoyed seeing shows and supporting music throughout their marriage. They saw *Cats* in Chicago when they lived in Beloit in the 1980s and Frank sought funding for the musical program at Beloit College. Cynthia Wong Stamberger interview, July 14, 2018, WFP.

41. Frank Wong letter to Mary Wong Palmer, October 5, 1967, WFP.

42. Frank Wong letter to Mary Wong Palmer, July 8, 1967, WFP. Frank and Cynthia were married before a judge and consular official in late July and then formally married on September 2, 1967. Cynthia Wong Stamberger interview, July 14, 2018, WFP.

43. Frank Wong letter to Mary Wong Palmer, February 15, 1963, WFP.

44. Worries expressed in correspondence with Mary Wong Palmer, WFP. Frank was twenty-nine years old when he met eighteen-year-old Cynthia Tsao in Taiwan. He was forty when his older son, Christopher, was born.

45. Frank Wong letter to Mary Wong Palmer, January 4, 1976, WFP.

46. Frank Wong letter to Mary Wong Palmer, July 19, 1963, WFP.

47. Frank Wong letter to Mary Wong Palmer, April 30, 1973, WFP.

48. Frank Wong letters to Mary Wong Palmer, April 28, 1967, March 16, 1975, WFP.

49. Frank Wong letters to Mary Wong Palmer, April 19, 1971, March 15, 1971, September 4, 1972, WFP.

50. Frank Wong letter to Mary Wong Palmer, August 31, 1970, WFP.

51. Frank Wong letter to Mary Wong Palmer, November 10, 1973, WFP.

52. Frank Wong letter to Mary Wong Palmer, April 30, 1973, WFP. The trip was financed with a grant from the Kettering Foundation. Cynthia Wong Stamberger said that Mrs. Snow had stayed with the Wongs when she visited her daughter in Yellow Springs, and they became friends. Frank asked Mrs. Snow to write to Premier Zhou Enlai for permission to visit, which he granted. Cynthia Wong Stamberger email to Mary Wong Palmer, May 29, 2018, WFP.

53. Terry Lee letter to Harry Wong, January 31, 2002, "Lee" folder, WFP.

54. 1974 postcard of the Peking Post Office, from Frank Wong to Mary and David Palmer, WFP.

55. Frank Wong Curriculum Vitae, August 27, 1987, University of the Redlands, in "Professional Career of Frank," WFP. Frank Wong's master's thesis (on Woodrow Wilson) and his dissertation are both available from the University of Wisconsin–Madison.

56. Frank Wong to Mary Wong Palmer, July 8, 1967, WFP.

57. Frank Wong, "The China Triangles," *Antioch College Review*, Winter 1969, WFP.

58. Relations were not normalized until January 1, 1979, but the Nixon visit in 1972 began the rapprochement.

59. Scott Hoober, "China's Struggle Held Fateful," *Beloit Daily News*, February 17, 1967.

60. "College Official to Visit China," *Beloit Daily News*, May 22, 1984. Fudan ceased sending students to Beloit, even while Beloit students continued to attend Fudan, after the Tian An Men Square protests of 1989; but Chinese students came to Beloit again beginning in 1997. The exchange relationship was ended in 2005. In 2015 a new relationship formed that allows students in Fudan's College of Foreign Languages and Literatures to study at Beloit College. Elizabeth Brewer, Director of International Education, Beloit College, email to author August 20, 2020.

61. Wong, "The American Experience in China."

62. Interview with Ian Nie, emeritus professor of music, June 5, 2020. See also Anand A. Yang, "Asian Studies Past, Present, and Future," *Asia Policy* 9 (January 2010): 21–25.

63. John Rapp's hire was decided on by the political science department, but he credits Frank Wong for placing a Chinese anthropologist on his hiring committee. John Rapp interview, August 21, 2020. Frank also encouraged summer theater and programs in music and fine arts. Mary Wong Palmer interview. He helped find funding for *Beloit Fiction Journal*, which continues today. Fred Burwell email to Mary Wong Palmer, summer 2020.

64. Ian Nie interview, June 5, 2020. Ian's family had immigrated to Beloit from Hong Kong in 1959, drawn by a longtime connection to Beloit Corporation. Ian Nie's family had owned a paper factory in Tianjin, China, that used Beloit Corporation machines.

65. Christopher's mother, Cynthia, remembered classmates called him "a Japanese" and asked whether he could see out of such small eyes. Cynthia Wong Stamberger interview, July 14, 2018, WFP.

66. Intra-Campus Memorandum from President James R. Appleton to the University Community, November 23, 1992, in "Frank's Professional Papers, letters, etc." folder, WFP.

67. Intra-Campus Memorandum from President Appleton to the University Community, 1995, in "Frank's Professional Papers, letters, etc." folder, WFP.

68. Frank F. Wong, "Diversity and Our Discontents," *American Association for Higher Education Bulletin*, October 1992, 1–5. See also Frank Wong, "Diversity's Challenge to Community," a speech delivered to the Western College Association Annual Meeting, April 2, 1991, in "Frank's Professional Papers, letters, etc." folder, WFP.

69. President of AACU Carol Geary Schneider lauded Frank and cited his foundational work in a 2011 AACU publication, "Drama of Diversity and Democracy," vii, https://www.aacu.org/sites/default/files/files/publications/DramaofDiversity_2011.pdf.

70. Mary Wong Palmer interview of Jerry Berberet, July 23, 2020. Berberet was the Association of New American Colleges and University's first executive director, from 1995 to 2006. Transcript of interview in WFP.

71. Frank Wong, "The Ugly Duckling of Higher Education," presented at the University of the Pacific, March 30, 1990, https://nacu.edu/wp-content/uploads/2019/01/Wong-Ugly-Duckling.pdf. The essay is marked "Wong's classic essay that started 'the conversation.'"

72. Mary Wong Palmer interview of Jerry Berberet, July 23, 2020, WFP.

73. Frank Wong obituary, in "Frank" folder, WFP.

74. In "Frank's Professional Papers, letters, etc." folder, WFP.

75. Mary Wong Palmer interview of Jerry Berberet, July 23, 2020, WFP.

76. Gim's role as surrogate father to the family continued for the rest of his life. Fourth-generation Alex Dereix said her mother, Wendy Wong Dereix, was influenced by Gim's model as a father, both as a surrogate father to his younger siblings and as father to his own children. Alex Dereix interview, July 29, 2020.

77. Mary explained that her grandfather had selected Chinese names for her older siblings Gim, Fung, and Ham (George). After he died they were given English names. But Yee Shee also called each of the younger children by a Chinese name that was not on the birth certificate.

78. Mary Wong Palmer interview, August 2020. Asked why she hadn't known that earlier, Mary suggested three reasons: no one wanted to revisit the tragedy that

caused Yee Shee such distress; the family members were so busy working that it never came up; and Chinese families do not discuss traumatic events.

79. ILS, a way for the University of Madison to offer a liberal education to a portion of its students, started for two hundred students in 1948. A grade point average was required to be accepted into the program. Mary Wong Palmer interview, August 2020. See also Richard L. Olson letter, https://ils.wisc.edu/wp-content/uploads/sites/135/2017/04/final_Olson_ILS_article_2014.pdf.

80. Shira Tarrant, "When Sex Became Gender: Mirra Komarovsky's Feminism of the 1950s," *Women's Studies Quarterly* (Winter 2005): 334–55, 335.

81. Only twenty women were selected for Mortar Board in their junior year of college at UW–Madison.

82. Mary Wong Palmer interview, 2010, WFP.

83. Frank Wong had also served on this committee. Mary Wong Palmer interview, August 2020.

84. Undated newspaper clipping, "Mary Wong Palmer" folder, WFP.

85. Helen McLean, the first Black teacher in the Madison School District, was passed over for a job when she applied in 1958. She said the hiring committee told her that white parents would not be comfortable with a Black teacher. McLean began working at Longfellow Elementary in 1961. https://madison365.com/history-black-madison/.

86. Daniel Gordon, "Legitimation, Ambivalence, Condemnation: Three Sociological Visions of the American University in the 1960s and 1970s," *The American Sociologist* 45 (March 2014): 51–67, 57.

87. Scholars of Asian American history refer to the relocation camps as American concentration camps, but Naomi Lidicker refers to the camp as a relocation camp. Mary Wong Palmer interview, March 12, 2021.

Chapter 6. Family Reunions

1. Ho, "Identity," 137.

2. Alex Dereix interview, July 29, 2020. For an insightful discussion of the importance of talking to siblings and other mixed-race persons while developing a mixed-race identity, see Stephen Murphy-Shigematsu, *When Half Is Whole: Multi Ethnic Asian American Identities* (Stanford, CA: Stanford University Press, 2012), especially 31–33.

3. Tim Rosenwong, PhD, second son of Frank Wong, is enthusiastic about the political activism and efforts of the young people he teaches in San Diego, California. Tim Rosenwong (a.k.a. Timothy Wong) interview, July 14, 2018.

4. Jon Way interview, July 15, 2018.

5. Gwen Neville, "Learning Culture through Ritual: The Family Reunion," *Anthropology & Education Quarterly* 15, no. 2 (1984): 151–66.

6. Robert Taylor, "Summoning the Wandering Tribes: Genealogy and Family Reunions in American History," *Journal of Social History* 16, no. 2 (Winter 1982): 21–37.

7. On Chinese associations in Chicago, see Ling, *Chinese Chicago*, 133–53.

8. Paul C. P. Siu, *The Chinese Laundryman: A Study of Social Isolation*, ed. John Kuo Wei Tchen (New York: New York University Press, 1987), 146.

9. There were two big box moments. Frank had popped out of a box at a previous reunion, at Yee Shee's birthday party in 1975. This time, he combined both the element of surprise for his young son, Christopher, and the ballad commemorating the family. Mary Wong Palmer interview.

10. Even so, one deficit of the play was the decision not to show that Yee Shee was despondent over Charles's death. The focus on her ability to surmount her difficulties also minimized them.

11. Wendy Wong Dereix email to second-generation siblings, 2013, in "Reunion Materials," Lisa Wong Fortsch.

12. "Grandma's Candy Dish" in "Reunion Materials," Lisa Wong Fortsch.

13. Wendy Wong Dereix email, in "Reunion Materials," Lisa Wong Fortsch.

14. "Brunch Schedule, 1982" in "Reunion Materials," Lisa Wong Fortsch.

15. Mary Wong Palmer notes, WFP.

16. Lisa Wong Fortsch email to group family members, September 8, 2013, WFP.

17. "MEMO from Harry to Marion, Fung, George, Jim, Frank, & Mary, RE: WONG FAMILY REUNION PROGRAM" in "Reunion Materials," Lisa Wong Fortsch.

18. Harry Wong email to author and other attendees, July 28, 2018, WFP.

Epilogue. Return to Mong Dee

1. Letter from Mary Wong Palmer to Terry Lee, January 27, 2009, WFP.

2. Jim Palmer interview, July 2018.

3. Mary Wong Palmer, "Visiting the Wong Village in China," October 25, 2008, WFP.

4. They had met the wife of Wong Chun-Kuen, son of Mary's grandfather's younger brother Wong Doo Won, in Guangzhou in 1984. Mary Wong Palmer interview, 2018.

5. See map in "Maps" folder, WFP.

6. Madeline Y. Hsu, "Migration and Native Place: Qiaokan and the Imagined Community of Taishan County, Guangdong, 1893–1993," *The Journal of Asian Studies* 59, no. 2 (May 2000): 307–31, 325–27.

7. Ibid.

8. Shari Palmer interview, July 15, 2018.

9. Cynthia Wong Stamberger email to Mary Wong Palmer, December 20, 2009, WFP. See also December 17, 2009, letter from the Consulate General in Los Angeles to Cynthia Wong Stamberger, WFP.

Index

References to figures and photographs appear in *italic* type; references followed by "n" indicate endnotes.

Admiral Oriental Line, *54*
American Association of Colleges and Universities (AACU), 118, 119
American Bowling Congress, 77
anti-miscegenation laws, 73–75
Antonsen, Emma and Charles (neighbors of Yee Shee Gok), 59, 178n30
Asian Americans, 129, 131–32, 184n3, 186n23; identity, 81, 93, 132, 190n2; internment camps, 190n87; intersectional identity, 97; provision against wives of Asian Americans in 1924 immigration law, 24, 53; in wartime U.S., 120, 186n29; women, 51–52, 97, 129
Association of New American Colleges and Universities, 119

Baker, Cherie Scholz (daughter of Fung Wong Scholz), 84, *84*, 140–41, 166n8, 182n36, 184n1
Beloit, Wisconsin, 30, 33, 42, 45, 47, 51, 59–60, 93–94, 117, 123–24, 134, 165n5, 173n16, 174n31, 178n21; growth and industrial production, 70; immigrant population, 59; map of, *38*; migrants from overseas and from U.S. South, 39–41; racial segregation, 41; racial stratification, 55–57
Beloit College, 3–5, 7, 55–57, 73, 75, 86, 111, 116, 135, 144, 165n2, 166n8, 178n26, 180n6, 180n8, 180n12, 181n21, 181n30, 187n40, 188n60
Beloit College Archives, 3, 5, 165n2, 166n6
Beloit College Chinese Students Club, 56–57
Beloit Corporation. *See* Beloit Iron Works
Beloit Daily News, 7, 55; article about George Wong, 89, *90*; article about Mary Wong, *125*; articles about race, 55–56; Frank Wong's first job, 7, 111
Beloit Historical Society, 5; honoring Yee Shee Wong, 66
Beloit Iron Works, 39, 70; George's career as engineering manager, 89, 92; Gim Wong as foundry engineer, 76
Berlin Machine Works, 39

Black Americans in Beloit, 104; Ida Mae Brandon Gladney, 40–41; racial discrimination against, 131, 178n21, 186n23, 186n24; Velma Bell, 174n23, 181n30

Bord, Avis (neighbor of Yee Shee Gok), 63, 121–22

Boxer Rebellion, 24, 27, 56; indemnity, 22, 56; indemnity students, 25

Cadet Nurse program: advertisement, 80; Fung Wong participating in, 79–81

Cantonese language, 27, 151

Chicago Chinese community, 26–29

Chicago Columbian Exposition (1893), 28, 39

Chinatown in Chicago, 27, 41

Chinese Americans, 53; choice of marriage partner, 73; claim of birthright U.S. citizenship for children, 25; gender balance among, 180–81n19; and Japanese and Japanese Americans, 186; mixed race, 132; second-generation, 9, 10, 69–70; third-generation, 143. See also Wong family

Chinese Cooking the Wong Way (Helen Wong Way), 100–101, 100

Chinese exclusion, 16–17, 26, 65–67, 101. See also Chinese Exclusion Act

Chinese Exclusion Act, 22, 24, 26, 28, 65–66

Chinese immigrants: in California, 23; in Chicago, 26–29, 170n40; immigration laws, 23–26; network of organized groups, 133–34; racism against, 23–24; second-generation and gender, 78

Chop House. See Nan King Lo Restaurant in Beloit, Wisconsin

Confucianism, 14, 34, 48, 49, 116, 176n2–4, 179n44, 187n37; as "social foundation" of Chinese family life, 48

Cultural Revolution in China (1966–1976), 115, 151, 176n2, 187n37; and Mao Zedong, 115

Dereix, Alexandra (granddaughter of Gim Wong), 131–32, 166n8, 189n76, 190n2

Dereix, Wendy Wong (daughter of Gim Wong), 75, 76, 140, 142, 166n8, 179n48, 180n10, 184n3, 189n76, 191n13

Dimock, Andy (son-in-law of Mary Wong Palmer), 140, 153–64

Erdman, Marion Marie. See Wong, Marion Erdman

Fairbanks, Morse and Company, 6, 39–40, 41, 70, 76

family knowledge, use of in history projects compared to paper sources, 5–6

Fam Nan Wah. See Liu Moi Han

foot-binding, 52–53, 67, 173n3, 177n14

Fortsch, Lisa Wong (daughter of George Wong), 5, 60, 89, 91, 91, 140–41, 166n8, 183n56, 183n60, 184n1, 184n3, 184n77, 191n11–14, 191n17; eulogy for father, 184n77

Freeman Shoes, 39

Gaelic (Pacific Mail steamship), 17, 18

Galloway, Lori Way (daughter of Helen Wong Way), ii, 99, 99, 101, 102, 143, 166n8, 183n68

Great Depression, 48, 60, 61, 67, 79, 97

Hoffert, Mary Scholz (daughter of Fung Wong Scholz), 42, 43, 84, 84, 166n8,

180n4, 182n41, 183n68, 184n2; Yee
Shee's oldest granddaughter, 84
Huang Guang-Han. *See* Wong Theong

immigration: Asian exclusion from, 67,
75; of Ben Yuk, 14, 16, 17–21, *18*, *19*;
Charles's application for Yee Shee,
35, *43*; of Charles to U.S., 33; Chinese
immigration to U.S., 22–26; and
Chinese women, 51–52; interview of
Doo Set, 29–30; laws in U.S., 2, 53
Immigration Act (1924), 177n18
interracial marriage in U.S., 9, 74
intersectionality, 97

Japanese Americans, 79–80, 106, 120,
128–29, 186n29

Lee, Catherine, 166n8
Lee, Ronald, 166n8
Lee, Terry (cousin of Mary Wong
Palmer), 73, 144, 146–47, 188n53,
191n1
Lee, Theresa. *See* Yih, Theresa Lee
Lidicker, Naomi and Bill, 128–29, 190n87
Liu Moi Han (mother of Yee Shee
Gok), 48, 50, *50*, 175n1
Lo Nanking Restaurant. *See* Nan King
Lo Restaurant in Beloit, Wisconsin

Madison General Hospital School of
Nursing, 79
McNeel, James H., 86, 182n48
Meyer, Julian J. and Adele, 37–39, 173n13
Mong Dee village (Taishan county,
Guangdong province, China), 29;
birth (1891) of Charles, 33; birth
(1870) of Doo Set, 14; Doo Set's new
house, 29; images of, *149*; map of, *15*;
marriage of Charles and Yee Shee,
34–39; Mary Wong Palmer's search

for, 144, 146–52; village gate (2008),
148; voyage from Mong Dee to San
Francisco, *34*; Yee Shee, 50–51, 57, 70
Morrow, Joyce Ann. *See* Wong, Joyce
Morrow
Moy, Gloria Wong (cousin of Mary
Wong Palmer), 144, 150, 179n41

Nakahiro, Jean. *See* Wong, Jean
Nakahiro
Nan King Lo Restaurant in Beloit,
Wisconsin, 7, 39, 41–42; Charles
and, 33, 41–42, 45–47; Gim Wong,
71; Great Depression impact on
business, 31, 60
nationalists, 27, 113; nationalist leader
Sun Yat-Sen, 53; nationalist army to
Taiwan, 113
Nie, Ian, 166n8, 188n62, 189n64
Noguchi, Alice, 79–81

Page Act (1875), 52
Palmer, David (husband of Mary Wong
Palmer), 7, *13*, 86, 99, 113, 124–29, *128*,
138, 144, 146, 149, 163
Palmer, James (son of Mary Wong
Palmer), 127, *128*, 146–48, *148*, 166n8,
191n2
Palmer, Mary Wong (daughter of
Wong Theong), 3–5, 7, *13*, 45, 51,
61, *62*, 63, *64*, 66, 86, 88, 89, 93, 95,
97, 99, 120–29, *121*, *122*, *125*, *128*,
137–40, 142, 144, *148*, *150*, 158–64,
166n8, 166n18, 170n35, 170n47, 176n6;
at 2011 reunion, 144; in Beloit
Memorial High School band
uniform, *122*; benefited from city
and state communities, 123–24;
career in education, 126–29; children
of, 127, *128*; correspondence and
relationship with brother Frank,

Palmer, Mary Wong (*continued*)
111–15; family history research, 3–4,
129–30, 152, 180n11, 182n46, 182n48,
182n50, 182n54, 183n57, 183n65,
183n69; at family reunion, 137;
friendship with neighbors, 128–29;
gaining recognition for leadership
ability, 125–26; identity, 120–21;
legacy, 129; marriage with David
Palmer, 124–25; in news clipping
about Youth Conference from *Beloit
Daily News*, 125; relationship with
family members, 121–22; schooling,
120–21, *121*; search for Mong Dee
village, 146–52, *148, 149, 150*; in
wedding of George Wong, 88
Palmer, Sharon "Shari" (daughter of
Mary Wong Palmer), 127, *128*, 166n8;
author of play at 2005 Wong family
reunion, 140, 146, 153–64, 166n8,
191n8
"paper son," 25–26, 31, 33, 38, 101

Qing Dynasty (1644–1912), 21, 24, 52,
116, 176n2

race and racism: against African
Americans, 55–56, 131, 186n23;
against Chinese immigrants, 24–25,
65–66, 67, 182n37; Fung Wong
experience, 82, 180n4; Gim Wong
experience, 70–71, 74–75, 180n4;
Harry Wong experience, 105–7, 108;
Helen Wong experience, 95, 97;
Mary Wong experience, 120–21;
racial stratification in Beloit, 55–57;
racial taunts, 180n4, 184n2; against
second-generation Chinese
American children, 69, 184n2
reunions of Wong family, 131–45; 2005
family reunion schedule, *142*; 2018

reunion, 5, 145; connections among
family members, 143–45; after death
of Yee Shee, 134, 135; family wisdom
and traditions, 135–43; play written
for 2005 reunion, 153–64; remem-
brance of past reunions, 131–33, 134;
Yee Shee and extended family at, *134*
Ring, Catherine Wong (daughter of
George Wong), 89, 91, *91*, 166n8,
183n68
Rosenwong, Tim (son of Frank Wong),
113, *114*, 117, 132, 138–39, 166n8, 190n3

Scholz, Alan Guy (son of Fung Wong
Scholz), 83, 84, *84*, 133, 166n8, 171n53,
182n39, 183n42, 183n68; Yee Shee's
oldest grandson, 83, *83*
Scholz, Cherie. *See* Baker, Cherie Scholz
Scholz, Elwood "Al" (husband of Fung
Wong Scholz), *13*, 82–85, *84*, 104,
166n10
Scholz, Fung Wong (daughter of Wong
Theong), 5, 6, *13*, 45, 46, 59, *61*, 62,
63, 64, *64*, 78–85, *81*, *84*, 142, 143, 158,
159, 160, 161, 163, 164, 166n8, 181n28,
184n2; Beloit Hospital emergency
room, 81–82; birth (1926) of, 57, *58*; in
Cadet Nurse program, 79–81,
182n34; Chicago rotation, 79;
children of, 84, *84*, 171n53, 180n4;
choice of marriage partner, 82–83;
community volunteer work, 85,
92; early job experiences, 78;
eldest daughter expectations, 78;
experience of racism, 82, 180n4,
184n2, 184n3; first Chinese American
woman seeking work in Beloit, 78;
friendship with Alice Noguchi,
79–81, 82; legacy, 85; lessons in
writing Chinese, 181n3; marriage
with Elwood "Al" Scholz, 82–84;

memory of father, 45–46; named by grandfather, 189n77; nursing school, 81, 182n35; parental role with siblings, 92, 120, 136, 159; primary caregiver for Yee Shee, 89; training as nurse in World War II, 79

Scholz, Mary. See Hoffert, Mary Scholz

Shitou village (Yee Shee's village), 48, 150

Smith, Arthur Henderson (China missionary, Beloit College alum), 56, 178n27

"social foundation" of Chinese family life, 48

Spanton, Ann Wong (daughter of Gim Wong), 75, 76, 144

SS *President McKinley*, 53, 54, 154

Stamberger, Cynthia Tsao Wong. *See* Tsao Ssu-ying, Cynthia

Taishan City, 15, 34, 146

Taishan county (Guangdong province, China), 14, 21–22, 48, 146, 151–52, 191n6

Tang, C. Y., 178n26

Toy, Susan Wong (cousin of Mary Wong Palmer), 146, 152, 170n47, 171n59, 171n2, 172n4, 173n16, 179n41

train route from Seattle to Chicago (1923), 55

Transcontinental Railroad, 23, 169n25

Tsao Ssu-ying, Cynthia (wife of Frank Wong), 4, 5, 13, 112, 114, 144, 152, 166n8, 173n14, 187n40, 187n42, 188n52, 189n65, 191n9; at family reunion, 139; interview with, 169n20; marriage with Frank Wong, 112–13, 112

University of Wisconsin–Madison, 5, 7, 9, 73, 76, 82, 86–88, 94, 96, 97, 105, 106, 108, 111, 115–16, 124, 125–27, 174n23, 179n45, 186n24, 188n55

Warner Instrument, 39

Wa Sam laundry in Beloit, Wisconsin, 42

Way, Helen Wong (daughter of Wong Theong), 3, 13, 61, 61, 62, 64, 75, 88, 94–102, 95, 96, 97, 99, 120, 125, 144, 158–64, 168n6; birth (1931) of, 60, 94; children of, 99, 99; *Chinese Cooking the Wong Way* (1977), 100, 100; choice of marriage partner, 95–96; and cooking, 100–101; correspondence with Mary, mother, and Fung, 185n5; death (1984) and burial of, 101–2; eulogies, 102, 185n21; experiences in Hawaii, 98; experiences in Washington, DC, 185n11; experiencing racism, 95, 97; family history, 3, 101, 129–30, 165n2, 167n6, 168n16, 172n4, 175n41, 185n22; at family reunion, 136–38, 144; intersectional identity, 94–98, 99, 185n18; legacy, 102; life in Pullman, Washington, 99–1004; marriage with James Leong Way, 97; roasted pig joke, 99; thriftiness, 97, 136, 185n14; University of Wisconsin–Madison occupational therapy program, 9

Way, James Leong (husband of Helen Wong), 13, 96, 97, 99, 102, 137, 144

Way, Jon (son of Helen Wong), 99, 99, 102, 132, 166n8, 183n68, 190n4

Way, Lani (daughter of Helen Wong) and Peter Lude, ii, 98, 99, 99, 101, 102, 142, 144, 166n8, 177n17, 183n68, 185n8, 185n13

Way, Lori. *See* Galloway, Lori Way

West, Stacey Wong (daughter of Harry
    Wong), 107, *107*, 166n8
West Side Presbyterian Church, 45–46,
    97, 107, 174n36
WFP. *See* Wong Family Papers at Beloit
    College Archives
Wong, Albert (cousin of Mary Wong
    Palmer) and Kathryn, 144, 149,
    170n46, 171n58, 172n4, 173n15, 173n16,
    175n47, 179n41
Wong, Ann. *See* Spanton, Ann Wong
Wong, Att (cousin of Wong Theong),
    46, 173n16
Wong, Ben. *See* Wong Mun Bin
Wong, Bill (son of George Wong) and
    Ann, 52, 89, 91, 183n70, 183n73; family
    website, 140; publication, 183n63
Wong, Bob. *See* Wong Mun Soo
Wong, Catherine. *See* Ring, Catherine
    Wong
Wong, Charles. *See* Wong Theong
Wong, Christopher (son of Frank
    Wong), 113, *114*, 117, 144, 166n8,
    187n44, 189n65, 191n9
Wong, Cynthia Tsao. *See* Tsao Ssu-ying,
    Cynthia
Wong, Daphne (daughter of Harry
    Wong), 107, *107*, 143
Wong, David (son of George Wong),
    89, 91, *91*, 166n8, 179n48, 183n58,
    183n68, 184n74, 184n76
Wong, Don (cousin of Wong Theong),
    42–44, 46–47, 175n41–48, 183n62
Wong, Frank (son of Wong Theong),
    3, 7, 13, 23–24, 61, 62, 64, 65, 95–96,
    95, 110–19, *112*, *114*, 135, 158, 160, 162,
    163–64, 179n45; at 1982 family
    reunion, 135–38, *135*; academic
    exchange in China (1974), 115,
    188n52, 188n54; academic exchange
    program between Fudan University
    and Beloit College (1985), 116;
    academic study of Chinese language,
    history, and politics, 115–16, 187n37;
    advocate of diversity on college
    campuses, 117; big box jest, 135–40,
    135, 191n9; birth (1935) of, 60; chil-
    dren of, 113, *114*, 190n3; commentary
    on changing culture and foreign pol-
    icy of U.S., 114–15; correspondence
    and relationship with sister Mary,
    111–15, 179n45; eulogy for Yee Shee
    Gok, 67–68; family history, 3–4,
    129–30, 174n39, 179n38; founding of
    New American Colleges, 118–19;
    marriage with Cynthia Tsao
    Ssu-ying, 112, *112*, 113; obituary of,
    189n73; professor of Asian history
    at Antioch College, 113–16; provost
    and vice president at Beloit College,
    116–17, 187n40, 188n63; provost and
    vice president at University of
    Redlands, 117–19, 189n66, 67;
    publications, 169n28, 188n57, 189n68;
    recognition from national academic
    organizations, 119, 189n69, 189n70,
    189n71
Wong, Fung. *See* Scholz, Fung Wong
Wong, George Ham (son of Wong
    Theong), 3, 7, 13, 60, 61, 62, 63, 64,
    72, *72*, 75, 85–92, 87, 90, 91, 105,
    116, 137, 138, 158, 160, 161, 163, 164,
    168n6; Beloit College attendance,
    7; *Beloit Daily News* article about,
    89, *90*; birth (1928) of, 57; career as
    engineering manager at Beloit Iron
    Works (later Beloit Corporation),
    89, *90*, 183n64; childhood of, 85–86;
    children of, 89, 91, *91*, 144, 183n67;
    correspondence with Joyce Ann
    Morrow, 88, *88*; family history, 3,
    129–30, 167n6, 168n16; family

visit during 2015 reunion, 183n70; goals of, 85–86; legacy, 89, 91; marriage with Joyce Ann Morrow, 88; memories of father, 45, 174n33; military service during Korean War, 86–87, *87*; named by grandfather, 189n77; parental role with siblings, 85; primary caregiver for Yee Shee, 89; University of Wisconsin–Madison, 86–87

Wong, Gim (son of Wong Theong), 7, *13*, 30, 45, *58*, *59*, 60, *60*, 61, *62*, 63, 64, *64*, 65, 70–78, 72, 74, 76, 79, 88, 93, 105, 138, 144, 158–64, 173n15, 186n27; Beloit College attendance, 7, 72–73, 116, 180n6, 180n8, 180n12; birth (1924) of, 53, 57, 70; career as industrial engineer, 76; children of, 75–76, *76*; choice of marriage partner, 73–75; death (1991) of, 76; desegregated sport of bowling, 77; education, 71, 73; employment, 76–77; experience of racism, 70–71, 75, 180n4; legacy, 77–78, 189n76; lessons in writing Chinese, 180n3; marriage with Marion Marie Erdman, 75, 181n21; memory of father, 45, 172n5, 173n12, 173n15, 174n33; named by grandfather, 189n77; in Nan King Lo restaurant, 47, 63, 71; primary caregiver for Yee Shee, 89; public office in Beloit, 76–77; relationship with mother, 73; role as surrogate father, 64, 71, 73, 85, 92, 95, 120, 180n5, 189n76; role model to his children, 77–78; service in U.S. Army, 71–73, 180n11; University of Wisconsin–Madison, 73; in wedding of George Wong, 88; with Yee Shee Wong in Hong Kong, 73, 74, 179n40; 180n15

Wong, Harry (son of Wong Theong), 5, 6, *13*, 60, 61, 62, 64, *103*, *106*, *107*, *110*, 132, 138, 144, 158, 160–64, 166n8, 166n10, 184n2; at 1982 family reunion, 144; anesthesiologist residency, *106*, 107; awards, 109–10; at Beloit Memorial High School, *103*; birth (1933) of, 60; black sheep, 103, 105, 108, 186n27; career in Salt Lake City, 108–10; children of, 107, *107*, *110*; choice of marriage partner, 105–7, 186n30; clinical teaching at University of Utah Medical School, 109; concern about mother, 102; in early age, 102–3; experienced racial discrimination, 105–7, 108, 184n2; with extended family, *110*; eye problem, 107–8; Harry Wong Presidential Endowed Chair in Anesthesiology, 109; hosts 2018 reunion in Salt Lake City, 145; industrial accident at Fairbanks Morse, 105; legacy, 109–10; life after retirement, 110; marriage with Jean Nakahiro, 107; memories of father, 45, 102; opens ambulatory surgical facility, 109; practice of anesthesiology, 108; publication, 187n32; schooling, 103; studying metallurgical engineering program, 105; University of Wisconsin–Madison engineering and medical studies, 105; work at Fairbanks, 103–5

Wong, Helen. *See* Way, Helen Wong

Wong, Jean Nakahiro (wife of Harry Wong), *13*, 106–7, *107*, 108, 110, *110*, 132, 138, 144, 145, 163, 166n8, 186n29

Wong, Jeffrey (son of Harry Wong), *107*, *107*, 108, 142, 166n8

Wong, John (son of Gim Wong) and
    Becky, 75, 76–77, 76, 140–41, 166n8,
    174n36, 178n34, 179n50, 181n20,
    183n68, 184n1
Wong, Joyce Morrow (wife of George
    Wong), 13, 88–89, 88, 91, 91, 138, 142,
    144, 163, 183n59, 183n70
Wong, Lisa. See Fortsch, Lisa Wong
Wong, Marion Erdman (wife of Gim
    Wong), 13, 75, 76, 137, 142, 144, 162,
    181n21, 191n17
Wong, Mary. See Palmer, Mary Wong
Wong, Michael (son of Gim Wong), 75,
    76
Wong, Richard (son of George Wong),
    89, 91, 144, 183n68
Wong, Robert (son of George Wong),
    89, 183n67
Wong, Stacey. See West, Stacey Wong
Wong, Steven (son of Harry Wong),
    107, 107, 132
Wong, Susan. See Toy, Susan Wong
Wong, Timothy. See Rosenwong, Tim
Wong, Yee Shee. See Yee Shee Gok
Wong Ben Yuk (brother of Wong
    Doo Set), 5, 14, 16, 18, 19; ancestor
    chart, 12, 13; death of, 21, 167n6;
    identity, 165n2; immigration,
    17–21; interview, 168n15, 171n60;
    recognition of U.S. birthright
    citizenship, 19–20, 169n33; in U.S.
    detention, 17–19
Wong Bing Yoke. See Wong Doo Set
Wong Bok Ngow, 170n35
Wong Chow (brother of Wong Doo
    Set, closest friend and business
    partner of Wong Theong), 33, 34,
    46, 51, 172n4, 173n15, 173n16, 175n40;
    ancestor chart, 12, 13
Wong Doo Foo (brother of Wong Doo
    Set), 173n16; ancestor chart, 12, 13

Wong Doo Hane. See Wong Ben Yuk
Wong Doo Set (father of Wong
    Theong), 6, 11, 11, 59, 167n6; ancestor
    chart, 12, 13; birth and childhood in
    Mong Dee, 14; at Charles and Yee
    Shee's wedding, 172n8; in Chicago
    Chinese community, 26–29, 170n40,
    170n45; death (1934) of, 32, 61; death
    (1934) of Mun Tai (son), 32; death
    certificate of Doo Set, 171n58; family
    in China in 1922, 29; identity, 14–17,
    21; immigration of sons, 30–32, 60,
    171n49; marriage history, 29; and
    "paper son" phenomenon, 26; perils
    of transnational success, 29–31;
    presumed burial site, 171n60;
    residence in San Francisco, 169n20;
    trips to U.S. in 1912 and 1915, 172n12
Wong Doo Sung. See Wong Chow
Wong Doo Won (brother of Wong Doo
    Set), ancestor chart, 12, 13
Wong Doo Yee (brother of Wong Doo
    Set), 168n18, 173n16; ancestor chart,
    12, 13
Wong Doo Yuen (brother of Wong
    Doo Set), ancestor chart, 12, 13
Wong family of Beloit, 3–10, 11, 16, 36,
    59, 61, 62, 64, 134; ancestor chart, 12,
    13; in Beloit, 61; community efforts
    to help, 123; efforts to uncover
    history, 3–4, 101, 129, 146, 179n38;
    reputation in 1950s Beloit, 93–94;
    strength against racism and tragedy,
    69, 95. See also reunions of Wong
    family
Wong Family Papers at Beloit College
    Archives, 11, 54, 165n2, 166n6
Wong Fung Me. See Palmer, Mary
    Wong
Wong Fung Sem. See Way, Helen Wong
Wong Gim Chow. See Wong, Harry

Wong Gim Fe. *See* Wong, Frank

Wong Gim Ham. *See* Wong, George Ham

Wong Gwang Han. *See* Wong Theong

Wong Gwong On. *See* Wong Bok Ngow

Wong Hop, 173n16

Wong Kim Ark, 25, 169n33,

Wong Kwong Hon. *See* Wong Theong

Wong Lai Fong (daughter of Wong Doo Set), *13, 31*

Wong Luck, 173n16

Wong Mai Lon (sister of Wong Doo Set), ancestor chart, *12, 13*

Wong Mun Bin "Ben" (son of Wong Doo Set, half-brother of Wong Theong), 5, 6, *13*, 28, 30–32, *31*, 44, 47, 51, 65, 165n2, 169n20, 171n49, 171n52, 171n58, 173n17; living with Charles's family, 57, 59

Wong Mun Nging "Bill" (son of Wong Doo Set, half-brother of Wong Theong), 5, 6, *13*, 30–31, *31*, 61, 158–62, 169n20, 171n49, 171n52, 171n58; living with Charles's family, 57, 59

Wong Mun Soo "Bob" (son of Wong Doo Set, half-brother of Wong Theong), 3, *13*, 16, 28, 30–31, *31*, 51, 167–68n6, 168n16, 171n51, 171n55, 171n57, 171n58, 176n6; arrival to U.S., 60

Wong Mun Tai "Tai" (son of Wong Doo Set, half-brother of Wong Theong), *13*, 28, 30–31, *31*, 51; arrival to U.S., 60

Wong Sang, 18, 19, 20, 168n11

Wong Soon Pon (paper father of Wong Theong), 33, 172n3, 172n12

Wong Theong (a.k.a. Charles Wong), 3, 7, 8, 9, *13*, 17, 30–31, 33–47, *44*, 49, 50–51, *58, 59*, 102, 140, 152, 154–59, 170n40, 172n5, 173n14, 173n16, 177n20; in California, 37–39; cars, 44, *44*, 174n33; certificate of identity, 35; children of, 177n9; Chinese government confirmation of name and ancestral village, 171n1; death (1938) of, 46–47, 175n41, *42*; immigration of Yee Shee, *43*, 51–55, 177n20; immigration to U.S., 33–34; life in Beloit in 1920s and 1930s, 57–62, 174n31; marriage with Yee Shee, 34–37, *36*, 172n8; mother's death, 171n2; Nan King Lo Restaurant, 41–42, *44*, 45–46, 63, 173n15, 173n16, 174n31, 174n39; in Ogden, Utah, 172n5, 172n12; as paper son, 38, 172n3; partnering with Wong Chow, 39, 46, 172n4, 173n15; property in Hong Kong, 46, 47, 175n40, 179n40; purchase of home in Beloit, 41–42, 51; siblings, 170n47; voyage from Mong Dee village to San Francisco (1909), 34, 172n4

Yates American, 70, 71, 72

Yee Shee (wife of Wong Ben Yuk), 21

Yee Shee (wife of Wong Doo Set), *31*, 171n2, 179n41

Yee Shee Gok (wife of Wong Theong), ii, *ii*, v, 3, 8, *13*, 30, *31*, 33, 48–68, *49*, *58, 59, 61, 64, 66*, 74, 83, 98, 105, 123, 132, 134, *134*, 140, 149–50, 154–64, 166n8, 177n20, 179n41; becoming literate, 51; birth (1894) of, 48; building community in Beloit, 57–62; children of, 30, 50, 57, *58, 59, 60, 61, 62, 64, 65, 134*, 189n77; death (1978) of, 66; duties of, 50–51; education level, 51; eulogy by Frank, 67–68; with Gim Wong in Hong

Yee Shee Gok (*continued*)
    Kong, 74; Grandma's candy dish,
    141, *141*; with grandson Alan Scholz,
    83; grief after Charles's death, 47, 63,
    122, 189n78, 191n10; honored among
    "Inspirational Women—Past and
    Present," 66–67; immigration to U.S.
    during Chinese exclusion, *43*, 51–55,
    67; legacy, 67; life after husband's
    death, 48–49, 62–63; marriage with
    Charles, 34–37, *36*, 50; in Mong Dee,
    31, 37, 50, 51; "Memories of Mother"
    (by Mary Wong Palmer), 178n31;
    with mother and sisters-in-law, *50*;
    naturalization as U.S. citizen, 65, 66,
    67, 179n47; opinion about children's
    marriages, 73–74, 82–84, 96–97, 107,
    186n29; parents and home village
    (Shitou), 35–37, 48, 49, 50, *50*, 150,
    175n1, 185n22; racial stratification in
    Beloit, 55–57; relationship with
    grandchildren, ii, *ii*, *83*, 84, 89, 101,
    132–33, 166n8, 182n41, 182n42, 183n68;
    sale of Hong Kong properties,
    64–65, 183n66; sale of restaurant, 63,
    71, 174n39, 179n38; surviving and
    thriving in Beloit, 62–68; unbound
    feet, 52–53, 67; values, 49, 62–64, 65,
    67–68, 120, 136, 142, 178n34, 184n1;
    voyage to Beloit (1923), 53–55,
    177n20
Yee Shee Wong. *See* Yee Shee Gok
Yee Soo Sum, 175n1, 177n10
Yee Suey Wah. *See* Yee Thien Wu
Yee Thien Wu (father of Yee Shee
    Gok), 48, 175n1
Yih, Bob (creator of family charts), 12,
    13, 166n8
Yih, Theresa Lee, 166n8, 180n14